# THE BATTLE OF MALDON

Edited and Translated by

Bill Griffiths

**Anglo-Saxon Books**

By the same author

*An Introduction to Early English Law*
*Alfred's Metres of Boethius*
*The Service of Prime*
*Anglo-Saxon Magic*

Published by
Anglo-Saxon Books
Frithgarth
Thetford Forest Park
Hockwold-cum-Wilton
Norfolk
England

Printed by
Antony Rowe Ltd.
Chippenham
Wiltshire
England

First Published 1991
Updated and Reprinted 1992
Updated and Reprinted 1993
Expanded and Reprinted 1996
Expanded and Reprinted 2000

A Cataloguing-in-Publication record for this book
is available from the British Library.

ISBN 0–9516209–0–8

# CONTENTS

# INTRODUCTION

The Battle of Maldon was fought on the 10th or 11th August (medieval authorities vary) in AD 991. The few indications of site in the poem suit the Blackwater estuary below Maldon where Northey Island is joined to the mainland by a causeway, passable at low tide. The Viking force (led by Justin and Guthmund, according to Florence of Worcester) would have been on Northey, the Anglo-Saxons (we might fairly call them the English) who were led by Byrhtnoth, the ealdorman or King's deputy (for Essex?), seem to have been positioned opposite on the rather flat, exposed land that forms the bank of the estuary here. In the course of the fighting, the Vikings somehow gained passage to the mainland where a pitched battle ensued. Byrhtnoth was killed, a large proportion of the English force fled (or simply withdrew and saved themselves?), and a small group of loyal warriors alone remained to fight to the death round Byrhtnoth's body.

The poem recording this falls roughly into two parts: the first details Byrhtnoth's direction of the battle and ends with his death in battle; the second records the names, thoughts and actions of those warriors that remained on the battlefield, determined to die with their lord rather than abandon him or give up the fight.

Their motive for doing so may be rooted in that Germanic tradition noted in Tacitus' *Germania* ch.14:

"In the day of battle, it is scandalous to the Prince to be surpassed in feats of bravery, scandalous to his followers to fail in matching the bravery of the Prince. But it is infamy during life, and indelible reproach, to return alive from a battle where their Prince was slain. To preserve their Prince, to defend him, and to ascribe to his glory all their own valorous deeds, is the sum and most sacred part of their oath."

Whether such ideas could have survived the centuries and changes in culture between Tacitus' time and that of Byrhtnoth has been doubted, and it is not impossible that the poet expanded this section from his own knowledge of what was appropriate to the heroic past — to show how people ought to behave in the present.

In the poem itself, the warriors are said to be fighting on to avenge their lord (almost as though to provide sacrifices for his spirit — Saxo, of a similar context, says "non... dignosque animo proscribat honores" — "did not deny fitting offerings to his soul"); or it may be their motive included the wish to save their lord's body for burial, an important ritual to any Christian who hoped to be resurrected. Lacking a leader, they reinforce each other's resolve to fight on with vows never to retreat. It is the details of this last stand that justify the poem as a whole, pointing out the model for co-operative action; and the heroism displayed practically outweighs the significance of the defeat and the cowardice displayed by some.

Quite possibly the poem was intended to inspire resistance to the Vikings, and to counter the policy of paying Danegeld that dominated the 990s; it could thus be seen as a political as much as a historical or heroic poem. Others date the poem to the early decades of the 11th century, and express less confidence in the accuracy of its detail. Of course, the poem is primarily a creative work, using history as a frame for verse whose impact is at the level of language and idea. But though the poem does not reach the height of the noblest Old English lyrics, it is constantly surprising how vivid and realistic it is, using the techniques of verse (especially direct speech) to recreate the action 'before our very eyes'.

The achievement is the greater when one considers the relatively simple language and technical resources being employed. Old English poetry (e.g. *Beowulf*) can be complex and opaque, but here a straightforward narrative style is employed, and even then it sometimes seems that the poet has a struggle to achieve formal alliterative lines.

Particularly, the requirements of alliteration can lead to words being pressed into use beyond their strict original sense. Thus the use of **hyse** ('young warrior' line 2 etc.) does not imply that the Anglo-Saxon side consisted of untried troops; **ord** (line 69) means line rather than point or forefront; it is uncertain why the people of Sturmer, far away from the battle, should be **stedefæste** (line 249); **yrhðo** (line 6) does not fully seem to imply cowardice here; **yrre** (lines 44,253) is a special inspiring kind of 'anger'; and **ofermod** ('pride, overconfidence' line 89) applied to Byrhtnoth may not involve the sort of criticism often attributed to it. To some degree

6

sense can be subordinated to metrical needs, something not uncommon in any formal structured poetry.

But the internal evidence has been much discussed; it can be more constructive to look outside the text.

Awkwardly, the *Parker Chronicle* has a dislocated entry for the event, in which the Battle of Maldon gives the appearance of being linked with a later campaign, in 994. The simpler entry in the other chronicles for 991 is as follows:

«991 In this year Ipswich was sacked and very soon after that Byrhtnoth was slain at Maldon. And in the same year it was first advised that we should pay tribute to the Vikings on account of the terrible things they were doing round the coast. That was in the first instance £10,000. Archbishop Sȳriċ [or Siġeriċ, of Canterbury] counselled this policy.»

There are some negative points here worth taking up: the Battle of Maldon is not called a defeat; there is no indication that Maldon itself was sacked afterwards; the payment instigated by Syric might well have been a local Danegeld to protect the South-East rather than East Anglia, and was not necessarily paid to the same group of Vikings that fought at Maldon.

Also of importance is the account in the *Vita Oswaldi*, believed to have been written by Byrhtferð at Ramsey Abbey about AD 1000, and therefore arguably as good evidence for what happened as the poem itself, even if originally in rather flowery Latin:

«After not many months had passed, there occurred another very fierce battle in the east of this famous region, in which the glorious duke Byrhtnoth played a major part, along with his soldiers. How marvellously, how manfully, how boldly he urged his warrior leaders to the fight, who, dependent on the mere elegant play of words, can possibly make clear? There he stood, tall of stature, towering over the others; the power of his hand neither Aaron nor Hur supported, but manifold piety towards God gave him strength, and he was worthy of it. He struck hard with his right hand [i.e. sword], oblivious of the swan-white hair of his head [i.e. ignoring his own age], for works of charity and the holy Mass strengthened him. With his left hand [i.e. shield] he protected the unheeded weakness of his own body, which prayers and good deeds made up for. And when this precious commander of the battle-field saw his enemies fleeing [?or falling — Latin **ruere**], and his own men fighting more valiantly than ever and killing the enemy however they could, then with the whole of his strength he began to fight for his homeland. There fell [in battle] an incalculable number on both their side and ours, and Byrhtnoth also fell, and the remainder [of his men] fled. The Vikings were also heavily wounded, so that they could barely manage to man their boats.»

Incredibly, there is no mention of a causeway at the battle-site or of any role played by the sea. The death of Byrhtnoth and the flight of much of his army is clearly presented, and is not incompatible with the second half of the *Maldon* poem. However, the bald unalleved charge that the men of Essex fled may have rankled. Could this assertion have been a prompting for the poem itself, with its emphasis on the positive courage shown? (The usual criterion for winning was the final possession of the battlefield — hence the frequent exhortations not to take a step backwards but always to go forward.)

A decidedly later, but still important account of Byrhtnoth's death comes in the late 12th century *Liber Eliensis*, written at Ely Abbey, a site specially linked to Byrhtnoth. Its details seem at first sight odd, but may hide valid original data:

«...on one occasion, when report reached him that the Danes had landed at Maldon, he met them with an armed force and slew them almost all on the bridge over the river... Four years afterwards [the Vikings] landed at Maldon under Justin and Guthmund, son of Stectan, with a view to avenging the slaughter of their fellow countrymen... They sent word to him that they had come to avenge them and should hold him a coward if he refused to join battle. Byrhtnoth, inflamed to a pitch of daring by this message, summoned his former companions in arms to aid in the enterprise, and with a few men-at-arms marched off to give battle... On his arrival neither the small number of his own force nor the multitude of the enemy dismayed him, but straightaway he fell upon them and fought with them desperately for fourteen days... There was a vast slaughter of the enemy, whom he well-nigh put to flight; but taking heart from the paucity of his followers they formed a wedge and hurling themselves forward like one man succeeded after huge efforts in cutting off his head as he fought. Taking it with them they fled to their own country. And the Abbot [Ælfsige of Ely], hearing of the issue of the battle, went to the field with some monks and seeking out the hero's body bore it back to the church and buried it honourably...»

(trans. Sedgefield)

According to the *Liber Eliensis* the monks of Ely recovered the body (but not the head) of Byrhtnoth from the battlefield and buried this benefactor in their own abbey. In 1769, during rebuilding, bones were uncovered that could well have been those of Byrhtnoth (without skull).

There are also two significant links with the poem here: the Latin **pontem** ('bridge') resembles the **Pantem** (river-name) of the poem, as Sedgefield pointed out; and the factor of Byrhtnoth's audacity is a feature in both accounts. But did the *Liber Eliensis* perhaps echo the poem, or did the poet use some account that came also to be preserved later in the Latin prose?

It is certainly worth considering the idea that in the *Maldon* poem two battles have been telescoped into one (cf. Locherbie-Cameron, 1984). The causeway episode seems almost complete in itself, and it is hard to see how the English could have lost in a such a position. The heralds, the lining-up of the armies, and the main engagement are the attributes of a formal land battle, and have no connection with the estuary site as such. It may be significant that the "joins" between these two elements prove the weakest and most debatable passages of the poem: lines 62–71 where the tide comes in and the two forces are left looking at each other; and lines 84–95, where Byrhtnoth's **ofermod** is invoked to bring the Vikings over onto the mainland.

We are told (in the *Liber Eliensis*) that a tapestry was made by Byrhtnoth's widow, Ælfflæd, and presented to Ely Abbey. Schwabe (1993) and others since, posit this as the source of the poem. If the tapestry had two main long panels, one showing Byrhtnoth victorious at a bridge, or river, or causeway, and the other showing the death of Byrhtnoth in full battle, has the poet's main (and least effective) role been to dove-tail these two images together?

Of Byrhtnoth himself we know only the briefest outline of his life. In charters of AD 956 he first assumes the rank of 'ealdorman' (suggesting he could well have been over 60 at the time of the famous battle). He is associated in signing charters with Ælfwine the ealdorman of East Anglia; both seem to have supported King Edgar in his campaign to extend

9

Benedictine monasticism. By the time of the battle of AD 991, Byrhtnoth was probably the premier nobleman in England, and his death then would have attracted widespread comment, as evidenced by the Chronicles.

The manuscript containing the poem, Cotton Otho A.xii, was one of those severely damaged in the fire of 1731. Before then, fortunately, a transcript was made (in about 1720), and this is now our sole authority for the text. Of the phonology of the language little more can be said with profit than that it is Late West Saxon, and the burned MS might thus have been written in the scriptorium of pretty well any monastery that followed (or tried to follow) the standardised spellings encouraged by the Benedictine Reform movement.

*Maldon* is one of a small group of 'battle' poems in Old English, Welsh and Old Norse, whose interrelationship is uncertain. It is not a genre obviously pioneered in Latin literature, and this may help account for the simplicity or directness of the diction, verse-patterns and sentence structure in the poem. This does not detract from and may even assist the vividness of expression, while making it an ideal piece for beginners of Old English to tackle.

If the poem originally occupied an eight-page quire of which just the inner six folios survive, then probably no more than fifty lines are lost at either end. The lack of the evidence of the complete poem has encouraged endless speculation as to its purpose and genre — in which I have inevitably joined — and this is patently harmless providing you are willing to accept that no final solution to such questions may ever be possible.

# NOTES ON OLD ENGLISH VERSE

## a. Note on Old English Versification

Poetry in Old English (OE) did not adopt the system of a fixed count of syllables to a line, or a fixed stress rhythm pattern in the line, or the practice of rhyme linking lines – these were developed in the Latin hymn, adopted early in Welsh verse, later in Medieval English verse, eventually predominating in all European poetries. Instead, the Anglo-Saxons, after the lead given by Cædmon, continued to use a Germanic verse structure, based on alliteration, and adapted this pattern to suit all manner of Christian subject material.

Alliteration is a linking of letter sound e.g. the 'f' in *folce* alliterates with the 'f' in *foldan*, or 'st' in *Sturmere* and *stedefæste*. Sometimes this is difficult to spot, because the stressed syllables do not always stand first in a word. Thus *forheawen* alliterates with *hilde*, *gehealdan* with *heardne* – the unstressed prefixes are disregarded. As well as each consonant alliterating with itself, any vowel can alliterate with any other vowel e.g. 'y' with 'a': *yrre* with *anræd*, 'o' with 'eo': *ord* with *eorl*.

This linking of sound is built up into a line structure in a pattern that has some firm elements, but is also more flexible than we expect (compared to standard rhymed verse). In the first half-line there should be one prominent alliteration, and can be two; this links with just one important alliteration in the second half of the line. Just as the alliteration must be in a stressed syllable to stand out, so too the alliterating word must be a significant one in the line, in grammar and meaning.
Thus:

> *wicinga fela   wiges georn* (line 73)
> *syllan sæmannum   on hyra selfra dom* (line 38)

In these examples it would be considered odd if *fela* alliterated and *wicinga* did not, or *hyra* did but not *selfra*.

It is also considered that there can be non-alliterating stresses in the line, to an ideal total of four regular stresses, of which two or three will alliterate. Thus:

*se wæs éald genéat    ǽsc acwéhte* (line 319)

However, lines can have less than or more than four stresses:

*þæt þu þine léoda    lýsan wílle* (line 37)
*Se flód ut gewát.    Þa flótan stódon géarowe* (line 72)

And the number and pattern of unstressed syllables and words surrounding the stressed elements can vary, giving a variety of rhythm to the line:

*Sende ða se sǽrinc* (line 134a) pattern: / x x x / x
*bord to gebeorge* (line 131a) pattern: / x x / x
*on flot feran* (line 41a) pattern: x / / x
*on urne eard* (line 58a) pattern: x / x /

While in much modern poetry, alliteration is an ornament, used for special effect, in OE verse it is structural, a convenient traditional way of constructing line-patterns. It is a flexible resource, giving variety of spoken rhythm. Only rarely does it become a technical resource – perhaps the group of lines alliterating in 'w' at 95 to 97 or even 98 is a form of emphasis or climax, for example.

## b. Note on Inflected Language

The ease with which we use Modern English can lead us forget that it is still an inflected language – that is words change their endings to convey shades of meaning. Thus *one egg* but *two eggs*, singular and plural; or the use of *'s* to show possession: *the cat's whiskers*. Verbs can use an -s in the present e.g. *he sits*, and all verb forms need some modification to be applied to the past e.g. *he sits* becomes *he sat*; *I live* becomes *I lived*. In Old English there are many more inflexions, and they played a more important role, rather as they still do in Modern German. Like the King James Bible, the present verbs have endings no longer in use: *he reapeth, he recevieth, thou hast, thou knewest.* In OE the present plural is in -ath e.g. *willað* (they wish); the past can be formed after a 'strong' model e.g. *stod* (he stood) or a 'weak' one in -(e)d e.g. *amyrde* (he marred); the past plural takes -on e.g. *stodon* (they stood). Because the OE verb conveys more information by its ending that its modern equivalent, it is not always necessary to have a pronoun with

12

it: thus OE *feaht* (line 281) means 'he fought', *bædon* in line 306 means 'they bade'; pronouns like 'he' and 'they' are not always present or necessary.

The nouns are equally complex. Even inanimate objects had a gender (rather as we can call a car or a boat 'she') – in OE they used masculine, feminine and neuter classes of nouns, each with slightly different endings. And the endings varied according to the role of the word in the sentence. The four cases were nominative (subject), accusative (object), genitive (possessive) and dative (indirect object). The best way to understand this is to study some examples:

*Nominative & Accusative:*

Subject and object are rarely distinguished in OE nouns, which could lead to confusion. A preference is already evident for 'sense order' – that is subject (the doer), then verb (the action), then object (the recipient of the action), e.g.

> *Byrhtnoð bræd bill* (line 163) – 'Byrhtnoth drew (his) sword.'

Sometimes this ideal word order is altered to suit the alliterative needs of the line:

> *bord ord onfeng* (line 110) – 'board point received' i.e. shield took spear-point.

> *stihte hi Byrhnoð* (line 127) – 'encouraged they/them Byrhtnoth.'
> (Here the verb has a singular inflexion, so it is Byrhtnoth doing the encouraging and *hi* means 'them' not 'they'.)

> *sloh Offa þone sælidan* (lines 285–6) – 'struck Offa the seaman.'
> (Here the *-ne* and *-an* accusative inflexions show the seaman to be the object of the blow.)

*Genitive:*

Used for possession as in Modern English:

> *Wulfstanes bearn* (line 155) 'Wulfstan's bairn.'
> *wicinga werod* (line 97) 'Vikings' troop' or 'troop of Vikings'.

Sometimes the genitive is used for the object of a verb:

> *Feores hi ne rohton* (line 260) – 'Of-life they took no heed'

And rarely after a preposition:

13

*wið þæs beornes* (line 131) – 'towards the man'

The common genitive endings are *-es* (masculine and neuter nouns singular) and *-a* (all nouns, plural).

*Dative:*

As indirect object:

> *Hi willað eow... garas syllon* (line 46) – 'They wish to-you... spears to-give.'
>
> *me þinceð* (line 55) – 'to-me it-seems.'

The dative is commonly used with a preposition:

> *ðeodne gehende* (line 294) 'to-his-lord near'
> *to hame* (line 292) – 'to home'
> *on wælstowe* (line 293) – 'on the battle-field.'

Rarely the dative is used for the 'object' of special verbs:

> *ne mihte... ænig oþrum derian* (line 70) – 'not could... any to-the-others do harm.'

The common forms of the dative inflexion are *-e* in the singular and *-um* in the plural. Occasionally *-on* for *-um* is found e.g. *on Norhymbron* (line 266) 'among the Northumbrians'.

## c. Note on Auxiliary Verbs.

Old English (as Modern English, in fact) has only two clear tenses: present and past. Other tenses and shades of meaning are constructed by using an extra element, an auxiliary (or supporting) verb. In OE the common auxiliaries are:

> *mæg* – 'can, is able';
> *sceal* – 'must, shall';
> *wille* – 'will, wants to, intends to'; and
> *mote* – 'may, is allowed to'.

These stand as the active (finite) part of the verb, in combination with a second verb in the infinitive form. The infinitive (ending in *-an*) is only one word in OE, but in Modern English has to be rendered by two:

> *A mæg gnornian* (line 315) – 'forever he-will-need to-mourn.'
> *we willað... grið fæstnian* (line35) – 'we are-willing... an-agreement to-

14

confirm.'

*hu hi sceoldon standan* (line 19) – 'how they had to-stand.'

*Feallan sceolon hæþene æt hilde* (lines 54–5) – 'To-fall are-expected heathens in battle' i.e. heathens are expected to lose.

Other verbs can follow a similar construction:

*Ne þurfe we us spillan* (line 34) – 'not need we each-other to-destroy'
*ongan þa forð beran* (line 12) – 'he-began then forwards to-carry...'

Sometimes a construction of this sort can carry over several lines: thus at lines 36–9, during the Viking messenger's speech, an auxiliary verb *wille* 'are willing to' (line 37) combines not only with the infinitive *lysan* 'to redeem' in line 37, but with *syllan* 'to render' in line 38, and *niman* 'to take' in line 39. In return, the Vikings *willaþ* 'are willing' to *gangan... feran... healdan* (lines 40–1) 'to go, carry, maintain.'

### d. Words in Apposition

In order to form verse lines, it can be useful to have extra or redundant material at hand to fill out lines with. Repetition in OE verse can be seen as a result of this need; or it may be that a slower pace, with some emphatic duplication, was considered to make the sense clearer.
Thus:

*Ælfwine þa cwæð, he on ellen spræc* (line 211) – 'Ælfwine then said, he courageously spoke...' (In which the two phrases are pretty well equivalent.)

*ham siðie, wende fram wige* (lines 251–2) – 'home should-go, turn from-battle'

(Two variant but self-confirming concepts, one used to complete an alliterating line in 'h', the other to open a new alliterating line in 'w'.)

*linde ahof, bord to gebeorge* (lines 244–5) 'he raised (his) linden (shield), board in protection.'

*Linde* and *bord* are in apposition (that is, have the same grammatical role in the sentence, are both in the accusative case); and they both mean 'shield'. *Lind* in particular is a poetic term, one of a range of alternatives available to allow more freedom when it came to finding an alliteration – but part of a poetic diction not made much use of in *Maldon*.

15

Dunnere appears first in line 255 as a name, and then as '*unorne ceorl*' in line 256 – not a new person, but a restatement of his grammatical role as subject, and a little extra information. Lines 255–6 could arguably be reduced to 'Dunnere spoke next;' and the question of what material is significant and what redundant calls into doubt the accuracy of some of this 'extra detail' – is it authentic or merely added to fill out lines?[1]

The problem here for the beginner is knowing enough about the inflexions to recognise which words parallel which, are in effect duplicate information, and which constitute new elements in the sentence.

## e. Compounds

Compounds – two nouns joined together to make one new noun – are a common resource of OE prose and verse, and useful in verse as involving an extra (secondary) stress that adds weight and interest to the line profile. Examples in *Maldon* are *wine-mæg* 'friend-kinsman', *wi-haga* 'battle-wall' i.e. line of shields; *gryre-leoð* 'terror-song'. Because of their compactness, compounds can convey information vividly and imaginatively; the use of compounds widens the range of alternative expressions: thus the *wicinga ar* of line 26 (alliterating on 'w') can become the *brimmanna boda* of line 49, alliterating on 'b'. Nonetheless, compounds are also a resource used sparingly in *Maldon*, and examples are traditional not invented.

## f. List of Changes in Edited Text

(E = Elphinston's transcipt)

line 4; *to hige* – for E: *t hige*

line 5 *Þa þæt* – for E: *þa þ*

line 10 *þam wige* – for E: *þā w....ge*

line 33 *hilde* – for E: *..ulde*

line 61 *we* – for E: *þe*

---

1 Whole half-lines can be formulas, part of the stock of common poetic composition e.g. *yrre and anræd* (line 42 – 'angry and determined') or *brad and brunecg* (line 163 – 'broad and glint-edged'). This again affects the accuracy of detail and *west* in line 97 could be an alliterative as much as a geographical term (see Metcalf 1970). In terms of tapestry origin, it could even mean left-wards, that is against the right-heading trend of the 'good' characters.

line 103 *feohte* – for E: *fohte*

line 109 *grimme gegrundene*: '*grimme*' supplied to provide opening stress to line.

line 113 *wearð* – for E: *weard*

line 116 *wærð* – for E: *wærd*

line 171 *gestandan* – for E: *gestundan*

line 172 *hæleð gemælde*: to supply second half to line.
(*gemælde* is found as second stress in lines 230, 244, and *mælde* as fourth stress in lines 26, 43, 210)

line 183 *þæt hi on wæle lagon* – for E: *begen lagon*
(The line lacks alliteration, as the (trans)scribe(r) has duplicated an earlier formula; Grein suggested *bewegen* ('slain') in the b-verse, but I posit a solution on the model of lines 279 and 300. For cross-alliteration cf. line 80.)

line 191 *ærndon* – for E: *ærdon*

line 192 *Godwine* – for E: *godrine*

line 201 *þearfe* – for E: *þære*

line 212 *Gemunaþ þa* – for E: *ge munu þa*
(The possibilities here are (*ic*) *gemune* (I remember) or *gemunaþ* (remember! – an imperative plural). The first has some possible resemblance to the opening of Byrhtnoth's speech (line 173), but the second option is more action-full and closer to the letter-forms in E.)

line 224 *ægðer* – for E: *ægder*

line 292 *crincgan* – for E: *crintgan*

line 297 *Forð ða* – for E: *forða*

line 300 *Wigelmes* – for E: *wigelines*

line 324 *oð þæt* – for E: *od þ*

line 325 *guðe* – for E: *gude*

# PRONUNCIATION

| | |
|---|---|
| **a** | short back 'a' as in after |
| **ā** | long back 'a' as in father |
| **æ** | short front 'a' as in patter |
| **ǣ** | long front 'a' rather as in bad |
| **c** | as in cat |
| **ċ** | as in cheese |
| **cc** | always 'ch' (ċ) |
| **cg** | as 'dj' (OE **bricg** = **bridge**) |
| **cn** | as 'k' + 'n' |
| **e** | as in bet |
| **ē** | as in fête |
| **f** | between vowels is pronounced **v**: (OE **ofer** = **over**) |
| **g** | as in go |
| **ġ** | as 'y' in yacht |
| **h** | at the end of a word and in the combination **ht** is breathed more strongly, rather as in Scottish lo**ch** |
| **i** | as in fit |
| **ī** | as in feet |
| **o** | as in hot |
| **ō** | as in hôtel |
| **r** | is always pronounced, even at the end of a word |
| **sc** | as 'sh' (OE **scip** = **ship**) |
| **þ** | symbol for 'th' as in **th**in or fa**th**er (capital form Þ) |
| **ð** | symbol for 'th' as in **th**in or fa**th**er (capital form Ð) |
| **u** | as 'oo' in soot |
| **ū** | as in flute |
| **y** | like a French '**u**'('**oo**' with rounded lips) |

The above guide is necessarily approximate; long vowels (marked with an over-line) are basically the sound of the short vowel lengthened; diphthongs (two vowels together) are pronounced as two vowels but somewhat smoothed together. Word-stress is on the root syllable (usually the first syllable), but seldom falls on prefixes like **ġe-**, **on-**, **a-**, **be-** etc. The alliterating stresses of the verse line are marked in the edited text by letters in bold type.

# PRÉCIS OF THE POEM

*(after Sedgefield)*

## Edited Text

## PREPARATIONS

...brocen wurde.
Hēt þā hyssa hwæne   hors forlǣtan,
feor āfȳsan   and forð gangan,
hicgan tō handum   and t[ō] hiġe gōdum.                      4
Þ[ā] þæt Offan mǣġ   ǣrest onfunde
þæt se eorl nolde   yrhðo ġeþolian,
hē lēt him þā of handon   lēofne flēogan
hafoc wið þæs holtes,   and tō þǣre hilde stōp;             8
be þām man mihte oncnāwan   þæt se cniht nolde
wācian æt [þ]ām w[ī]ġe   þā hē tō wǣpnum fēng.
Ēac him wolde Ēadrīċ   his ealdre ġelǣstan,
frēan tō ġefeohte:   ongan þā forð beran                    12
gār tō gūþe – hē hæfde gōd ġeþanc
þā hwīle þe hē mid handum   healdan mihte
bord and brād swurd;   bēot hē ġelǣste
þa hē ætforan his frēan   feohtan sceolde.                  16
Ðā þǣr Byrhtnōð ongan   beornas trymian:
rād and rǣdde,   rincum tǣhte
hū hī sceoldon standan   and þone stede healdan,
and bæd þæt hyra randan   rihte hēoldon                     20
fæste mid folman,   and ne forhtedon nā.
Þā hē hæfde þæt folc   fæġere ġetrymmed,
hē līhte þā mid lēodon   þǣr him lēofost wæs
þǣr hē his heorðwerod   holdost wiste.                      24

20

## Literal Translation

### PREPARATIONS

...broken was.
He-bade then warriors' each / horse↓ to-abandon
far-away to-drive / & forward to-march,
to-think on hands / & on mind worthy.
When it↓ Offa's kinsman↑ / first discovered
that the earl would-not / lack-of-spirit↓ tolerate,
he allowed ( ) then from (his) wrists / cherished↓ to-fly
hawk↓ toward the wood, / & to the battle advanced;
by that one could know / that the youth would-not
weaken in the fight / when he to (his) weapons took.
Like him wished Eadric↑ / his master↓ to-serve,
lord↓ in battle; / he-began then forward to-bear
spear to combat – / he had proper appreciation
[for] that time that he with hands / hold could
shield & broad sword, / vow↓ he fulfilled
when he in-front-of his master / to-fight needed.
Then there B. began / men↓ to-arrange;
he-rode & instructed, / soldiers↓ he-taught
how they should stand / & the position↓ hold,
& required that their round-shields↓ / correctly they-held,
firmly by hand, / & not be-frightened not-at-all.
When he had that army↓ / carefully arranged,
he alighted then with [the] people / there to-him dearest it-was
where he his hearth-troop↓ / loyalest↓ knew.

# THE CHALLENGES

Þā stōd on stæðe,   stīðlīċe clypode
Wīcinga ār,   wordum mǣlde.
Sē on bēot ābēad   brimlīþendra
ǣrænde tō þām eorle   þǣr hē on ōfre stōd:   28
«Mē sendon tō þē   sǣmen snelle,
hēton ðē secgan   þæt þū mōst sendan raðe
bēagas wið ġebeorge,   and ēow betere is
þæt ġē þisne gārrǣs   mid gafole forġyldon   32
þon wē swā hearde   [hi]lde dǣlon.
Ne þurfe wē ūs spillan   ġif ġē spēdaþ tō þām:
wē willað wið þām golde   grið fæstnian;
ġyf þū þat ġerǣdest,   þe hēr rīcost eart,   36
þæt þū þīne lēoda   lȳsan wille,
syllan sǣmannum   on hyra sylfra dōm
fēoh wið frēode   and niman frið æt ūs,
wē willaþ mid þām sceattum   ūs tō scype gangan,   40
on flot fēran   and ēow friþes healdan.»
Byrhtnōð maþelode,   bord hafenode,
wand wācne æsc,   wordum mǣlde,
yrre and ānrǣd   āġeaf him andsware:   44
«Gehȳrst þū sǣlida,   hwæt þis folc seġeð?
Hī willað ēow tō gafole   gāras syllan,
ǣttrynne ord   and ealde swurd,
þā hereġeatu þe ēow   æt hilde ne dēah!   48
Brimmanna boda,   ābēod eft onġēan,
seġe þīnum lēodum   miccle lāþre spell,
þæt hēr stynt unforcūð   eorl mid his werode
þe wile ġealgean   ēþel þysne,   52
Æþelredes eard,   ealdres mīnes
folc and foldan.   Feallan sceolon

## THE CHALLENGES

Then stood on shore, / stridently called-out
Vikings' herald↑, / in-words spoke;
he in menace announced / sea-farers'
embassy to the earl / where he on bank stood:
"Me↓ sent to you / seamen↑ valiant↑,
ordered [me] you↓ to-tell / that you ought to-send speedily
treasures for safety; / & for-you better it-is
that you↑ this spear-attack↓ / with tribute bought-off
than we so fiercely / war↓ deal-out.
Not need we ourselves↓ destroy / if you are-rich to that [degree];
we are-willing for the gold / a-truce↓ to-confirm;
if you↑ it↓ will-decide, / who here most-important are,
that you↑ your people↓ / to-redeem wish,
to-give to-[the]-seamen / on their own reckoning
money for concord / & to-accept peace from us,
we are-willing with the coins / for-our-part to [the] ship to-go,
on sea to-travel / & with-you peace↓ to-keep."
B. spoke / shield↓ he-raised,
he-shook slender ash-[spear], / in-words spoke,
fierce & single-minded / he-gave them answer:
"Hear you, seafarer, / what this army is-saying?
They want to-you as tribute / spears↓ to-send,
poisonous point↓ / & old swords↓,
the heriot which you / in battle not will-profit.
Seamen's envoy, / go-announce again back-there,
tell to-your people / [a] much nastier tale,
that here stands unabashed / [the] earl with his troop,
who intends to-defend / (this) homeland ( ),
Æthelred's country, / (my) lord's ( )
people & land. / Fall must

hæþene æt hilde!  Tō hēanliċ mē þinċeð
þæt ġē mid ūrum sceattum  tō scype gangon                56
unbefohtene  nū ġē þus feor hider
on ūrne eard  in becōmon;
ne sceole ġe swā sōfte  sinċ ġegangan:
ūs sceal ord and ecg  ǣr ġesēman,                        60
grim gūðplega,  ǣr [w]ē gofol syllon!»

## AT THE FORD

Hēt þā bord beran,  beornas gangan
þæt hī on þām ēasteðe  ealle stōdon.
Ne mihte þǣr for wætere  werod tō þām ōðrum              64
þǣr cōm flōwende  flōd æfter ebban;
lucon lagustrēamas;  tō lang hit him þūhte
hwænne hī tōgædere  gāras bēron.
Hī þǣr Pantan strēam  mid prasse bestōdon,               68
Ēastseaxena ord  and se æschere;
ne mihte hyra ǣniġ  ōþrum derian
būton hwā þurh flānes flyht  fyl ġenāme.
Se flōd ūt ġewāt –  þā flotan stōdon ġearowe,            72
Wīcinga fela,  wīġes ġeorne.
Hēt þā hæleða hlēo  healdan þā bricge
wigan wīġheardne  sē wæs hāten Wulfstān,
cāfne mid his cynne;  þæt wæs Cēolan sunu                76
þe ðone forman man  mid his francan ofsċēat
þe þǣr baldlīcost  on þā bricge stōp.
Þǣr stōdon mid Wulfstāne  wigan unforhte,
Ælfere and Maccus,  mōdiġe twēġen,                       80
þā noldon æt þām forda  flēam ġewyrcan,
ac hī fæstlīċe  wið ðā fȳnd weredon
þā hwīle þe hī wǣpna  wealdan mōston.
Þā hī þæt ongēaton  and ġeorne ġesāwon                   84

heathens↑ in battle. / Too shameful to-me it-seems
that you with our coins / aboard ship should-go
un-fought-with / now you so far hither
into our country / in-[land?] have-come;
not should you so easily / treasure↓ gain:
us↓ must point↑ & edge↑ / first decide-between,
serious war-play↑, / before we↑ tribute↓ give."

## AT THE FORD

He-bade [them] then shields to-carry, / soldiers↓ to-advance
so-that they on the river-bank / all stood.
Not might there for water / [one] troop [get] to the other
where came flooding-in / tide↑ after ebb –
locked-tight [the] water-currents↑; / too long it-to-them seemed
[till] when they together / spears↓ could-carry.
They↑ there Pant's current / with powerful-display stood-next,
East-Saxons' battle-front↑ / & the ash-army↑[=V.].
Not could ( ) any (of them) / [the] others↓ harm
except who by arrow's flight / [his] end↓ received.
The tide ( ) moved (out). / The sailors stood prepared,
of-Vikings many, / for-war eager.
Told then heroes' guard↑ [B.] / to-defend the bridge
warrior↓ war-tough / who was called Wulfstan,
brave like his kin, / he was C.'s son
who the leading man↓ / with his spear shot-down
who there so-boldly / onto the bridge stepped.
There stood with Wulfstan / warriors↑ unafraid,
Ælfhere & Maccus, / spirited pair,
who would-not at the ford / flight↓ commit,
but themselves↓ steadfastly / against the foes defended
for-that time that they↑ weapons↓ / wield might.
When they [=V.] it↓ understood / & fully perceived

þæt hī þǣr bricgweardas   bitere fundon,
ongunnon lyteġian þā   lāðe ġystas,
bǣdon þæt hī upgangan   āgan mōston,
ofer þone ford faran,   fēþan lǣdan.                     88
Ðā se eorl ongan   for his ofermōde
ālȳfan landes tō fela   lāþere ðēode;
ongan ċeallian þā   ofer cald wæter
Byrhtelmes bearn;   beornas ġehlyston:                   92
«Nū ēow is ġerȳmed,   gāð riċene tō ūs,
guman tō gūþe!   God āna wāt
hwā þǣre wælstōwe   wealdan mōte.»

## THE BATTLE STARTS

Wōdon þā wælwulfas,   for wætere ne murnon,             96
Wīcinga werod   west ofer Pantan
ofer scīr wæter   scyldas wēgon;
lidmen tō lande   linde bǣron.
þǣr onġēan gramum   ġearowe stōdon                      100
Byrhtnōð mid beornum:   hē mid bordum hēt
wyrcan þone wīhagan   and þæt werod healdan
fæste wið fēondum.   Þā wæs f[e]ohte nēh,
tīr æt ġetohte;   wæs sēo tīd cumen                     104
þæt þǣr fǣġe men   feallan sceoldon.
Þǣr wearð hrēam āhafen,   hremmas wundon,
earn ǣses ġeorn – wæs on eorþan ċyrm!
Hī lēton þā of folman   fēolhearde speru                108
[grimme] ġegrundene   gāras flēogan.
Bogan wǣron bysiġe;   bord ord onfēng;
biter wæs se beadurǣs.   Beornas fēollon,
on ġehwæðere hand   hyssas lāgon.                       112
Wund wear[ð] Wulfmǣr,   wælrǣste ġeċēas;
Byrhtnōðes mǣġ,   hē mid billum wearð,

26

that they there bridge-guards↓ / fierce↓ had-found,
began to-dissemble then / [the] horrible strangers↑;
asked that they up-passage↓ / have might,
across the ford travel, / foot-troops↓ bring-through.
Then the earl began / on-account-of his over-confidence
to-allow of-land too much / to-the-hateful people;
began to-call-out then / across [the] chilly water
Byrhthelm's son↑ [=B.]; / [the] men [=V.] listened:
"Now for-you it-is opened-up, / come speedily to us,
men into war! / God alone knows
who the slaughter-site / win-control-of may."

## THE BATTLE STARTS

Advanced then death-wolves, / about water not cared-they,
Vikings' army, / west over [the] Pant,
over [the] shiny water / shields↓ carried,
fleet-men↑ to land / linden-[shields]↓ bore.
There opposite the-fierce-ones / ready stood
B.↑ with [his] men. / He with shields ordered [them]
to-form the war-wall / & [told] the army to-hold
firm against [the] foes. / Then was battle near,
glory in combat; / was the time come
that there doomed men / fall must.
There was [a] screeching raised, / ravens circled,
[& the] eagle for-food keen; / was on [the] ground uproar↑!
They let then from hands / file-hard spears↓,
cruelly sharpened / shafts↓ fly.
Bows were busy, / shield↑ weapon-point↓ received;
fierce was the war-charge. / Men fell,
on either side / warriors lay.
Wounded was W., / death-repose he-had-to-accept,
B.'s kinsman; / he with blades was,

27

his swustersunu, swīðe forhēawen.
Þǣr wær[ð] Wīcingum wiþerlēan āgyfen:        116
ġehȳrde iċ þæt Ēadweard ānne slōge
swīðe mid his swurde – swenges ne wyrnde –
þæt him æt fōtum fēoll fǣġe cempa.
Þæs him his ðēoden þanc ġesǣde        120
þām būrþēne þā hē byre hæfde.
Swā stemnetton stīðhicgende
hysas æt hilde, hogodon ġeorne
hwā þǣr mid orde ǣrost mihte        124
on fǣġean men feorh ġewinnan,
wigan mid wǣpnum. Wæl fēol on eorðan;
stōdon stædefæste. Stihte hī Byrhtnōð,
bæd þæt hyssa ġehwylċ hogode tō wīġe        128
þe on Denon wolde dōm ġefeohtan.

## BYRHTNOTH FIGHTS AND DIES

Wōd þā wīġes heard, wǣpen ūp āhōf,
bord tō ġebeorge, and wið þæs beornes stōp;
ēode swā ānrǣd eorl tō þām ċeorle,        132
ǣġþer hyra ōðrum yfeles hogode.
Sende ðā se sǣrinċ sūþerne gār
þæt ġewundod wearð wiġena hlāford:
hē sċēaf þā mid ðām scylde, þæt se sċeaft tōbærst        136
and þæt spere sprengde þæt hit sprang onġēan.
Ġegremod wearð se gūðrinċ: hē mid gāre stang
wlancne Wīcing þe him þā wunde forġeaf.
Frōd wæs se fyrdrinċ: hē lēt his francan wadan        140
þurh ðæs hysses hals – hand wīsode
þæt hē on þām fǣrsċeaðan feorh ġerǣhte.
Ðā hē ōþerne ofstlīċe sċēat
þæt sēo byrne tōbærst: hē wæs on brēostum wund        144

his sister's-son, / brutally cut-down.
There was to-the-Vikings / [a] requital given:
heard I that Edward / one↓ struck
hard with his sword – / stroke↓ ( ) he-withheld (not) –
so-that ( ) at (his) feet fell / [a] doomed warrior.
For-this to-him his lord / thanks spoke,
to-the chamberlain, / when he opportunity↓ had.
So stood-firm / [the] strong-minded↑,
warriors↑ in battle, / they-competed keenly [to see]
who there with weapon-point / first could
of [some] fated man / [the] life↓ gain,
of-some-warrior by [their] weapons. /[The] dying fell to earth;
stood [the] resolute↑. / Encouraged them B.↑,
said that warriors' each / should-concentrate on [the] fight,
who over [the] Danes wished / glory↓ to-achieve.

## BYRHTNOTH FIGHTS AND DIES

Advanced then war's bold-one [B.], / weapon↓ up he-raised,
shield in defence, / & towards some soldier stepped;
went thus resolute / [the] earl to the churl;
each [towards] their other / evil↓ intended.
Sent then the seaman↑ / [a] southern spear
so-that wounded was / warriors' lord [B.];
he [B.] banged then with the shield / so the shaft broke
& the spear↓ he-shook / so-that it sprang out.
Incensed was the war-man [B.]: he with spear stabbed
[the] proud Viking / who him the wound had-given.
Skilful was the fyrd-man [B.]: / he made his lance go
through the warrior's neck – / [his] hand guided [it]
so-that he↑ in that quick-attacker / [the] life↓ reached.
Then he [a] second↓ / immediately shot at
that the [V.'s] mail-coat burst: / he was in chest wounded

29

þurh ðā hringlocan;   him æt heortan stōd
ætterne ord.   Se eorl wæs þē blīþra:
hlōh þā mōdi man,   sæde Metode þanc
ðæs dæġweorċes   þe him Drihten forġeaf.                    148
Forlēt þā drenga sum   daroð of handa
flēogan of folman   þæt sē tō forð ġewāt
þurh ðone æþelan   Æþelredes þeġen.
Him be healfe stōd   hyse unweaxen,                          152
cniht on ġecampe:   sē full cāflīċe
bræd of þām beorne   blōdiġne gār:
Wulfstānes bearn,   Wulfmær se ġeonga,
forlēt forheardne   faran eft onġēan;                        156
ord in ġewōd   þæt sē on eorþan læġ
þe his þēoden ær   þearle ġeræhte.
Ēode þā ġesyrwed   secg tō þām eorle:
hē wolde þæs beornes   bēagas ġefecgan,                      160
rēaf and hringas   and ġerēnod swurd.
Ðā Byrhtnōð bræd   bill of sceðe,
brād and brūneccg   and on þā byrnan slōh.
Tō raþe hine ġelette   lidmanna sum                          164
þā hē þæs eorles   earm āmyrde.
Fēoll þā tō foldan   fealohilte swurd,
ne mihte hē ġehealdan   heardne mēċe,
wæpnes wealdan.   Þā ġȳt þæt word ġecwæð                    168
hār hilderinċ:   hyssas bylde,
bæd gangan forð   gōde ġefēran.
Ne mihte þā on fōtum leng   fæste ġest[a]ndan.
Hē tō heofenum wlāt,   [hæleð ġemælde:]                      172
«Geþance þē,   ðēoda Waldend,
ealra þæra wynna   þe iċ on worulde ġebād.
Nū iċ āh, milde Metod,   mæste þearfe
þæt þū mīnum gāste   gōdes ġeunne,                          176

30

through the chain-mail; ( ) in (his) heart stood
[the] deadly point↑. / The earl was the happier:
laughed then [the] valiant man, / spoke to-God thanks
for-the day's-work / that to-him [the] Lord had-granted.
Loosed then of-Vikings one↑ / javelin↓ from hand,
flying from wrist, / so-that it too successfully went,
into the noble / ( ) thane (of Æthelred) [B.].
( ) By (his) [B.'s] side stood / warrior half-grown,
[a] youth in battle: / he very boldly
drew from the man [B.] / [the] bloody spear;
W.'s son, / Wulfmær the younger
sent [the] very-hard [spear] / travelling back again;
point in went / so-that he on [the] ground lay
who his [W.'s] lord↓ before / so-grievously had-got-at.
Went then armoured / fellow [a V.][up] to the earl:
he intended the hero's / valuables↓ to-grab,
war-garb↓ & rings↓ / & patterned sword↓.
Then B. drew / blade from sheath,
broad & shiny-edged, / & on the mail-coat struck.
Too speedily him prevented / of-seamen one↑
when he the earl's / arm damaged.
Fell then to earth / tawny-hilted sword↑;
not could he keep-hold-of / hard blade,
weapon↓ control. / Then yet some speech↓ uttered
grey-haired war-man↑ [B.]: / soldiers↓ he-encouraged,
told to-go onward / [his] worthy comrades↓.
Not could-he then on feet any-longer / firmly stand.
He to heaven gazed, / hero↑ spoke:
"I-thank you, / Nations' Ruler [=God]
for-all those successes / that I in [this] life have-had.
Now I have, kind Maker, / utmost need
that you to-my soul / [a] favour↓ should-grant,

31

þæt mīn sawul tō ðē sīðian mōte
on þīn ġeweald, Þēoden engla,
mid friþe ferian.  Iċ eom frymdi tō þē
þæt hī helsceaðan  hȳnan ne mōton!»     180
Ðā hine hēowon  hǣðene scealcas,
and bēġen þā beornas  þe him biġ stōdon,
Ælfnōð and Wulmǣr, [þæt hī on wæle] lāgon
ðā onemn hyra frēan  feorh ġesealdon.     184

## GODRIC'S FLIGHT

Hī bugon þā fram beaduwe  þe þǣr bēon noldon!
Þǣr wurdon Oddan bearn  ǣrest on flēame,
Godrīċ fram gūþe,  and þone gōdan forlēt
þe him mæniġne oft  mēar ġesealde;     188
hē ġehlēop þone eoh  þe āhte his hlāford,
on þām ġerǣdum  þe hit riht ne wæs.
And his brōðru mid him  bēġen ær[n]don,
God[w]ine and Godwīġ;  gūþe ne ġȳmdon     192
ac wendon fram þām wīġe  and þone wudu sōhton;
flugon on þæt fæsten  and hyra fēore burgon,
and manna mā  þonne hit ǣniġ mǣð wǣre,
ġyf hī þā ġeearnunga  ealle ġemundon     196
þe hē him tō duguþe  ġedōn hæfde.
Swā him Offa on dæġ  ǣr āsǣde
on þām meþelstede  þā hē ġemōt hæfde,
þæt þǣr mōdelīċe  manega sprǣcon     200
þe eft æt þ[ea]r[f]e  þolian noldon.

## THE STAND

Þā wearð āfeallen  þæs folces ealdor,
Æþelredes eorl;  ealle ġesāwon
heorðġenēatas þæt hyra heorra læġ.     204

that my soul to you / travel might,
into your dominion, / Lord of-angels,
with peace journey. / I am petitioning to you
that it↓ hell-enemies↑ / bring-low ( ) should (not)!"
Then him↓ cut-down / heathen men↑,
& both the warriors↓ / that ( ) next-to (him) stood,
A. & W., / so-that they among [the] dead lay
when alongside their lord / life↓ they-gave-up.

## GODRIC'S FLIGHT

They fled then from battle / that there to-be wished-not!
There were O.'s sons / first in flight,
G. away-from war, / & that worthy [B.↓] abandoned
who to-him many↓ often / [a] mare↓ had-given;
he leapt-onto that horse / that↓ owned his lord↑,
in those trappings / which it right not was [to use];
& his brothers with him / both dashed-off,
Godwine & Godwig, / for-battle not cared-they
but they-turned-away from the fighting / & the forest↓ sought,
they-fled to that refuge / & their life↓ saved,
& of-men more↑ [went] / than there any fitness was
if they the favours↓ / all remembered
that he [B.] ( ) to (their) benefit / ( ) had (done).
So to-them O. in [the] day / earlier had-said
at the counsel-place / when he [B.?] [a] meeting↓ held,
that there bravely / many had-spoken
who afterwards at need / endure would-not.

## THE STAND

Then was fallen / the army's leader↑,
Æ.'s earl [B.]; / all↑ saw
hearth-officers↑ / that their commander lay [dead].

Þā ðǣr wendon forð   wlance þeġenas,
unearge men,   efston ġeorne:
hī woldon þā ealle   ōðer twēga,
līf forlǣtun   oððe lēofne ġewrecan.                    208
Swā hī bylde forð   bearn Ælfrīces,
wiga wintrum ġeong,   wordum mǣlde;
Ælfwine þā cwæð,   hē on ellen sprǣċ:
«Gemun[aþ] þā mǣla   þe wē oft æt meodo sprǣcon     212
þonne wē on benċe   bēot āhōfon,
hæleð on healle,   ymbe heard ġewinn.
Nū mæġ cunnian   hwā cēne sȳ!
Iċ wylle mīne æþelo   eallum ġecȳþan,               216
þæt iċ wæs on Myrcon   miccles cynnes;
wæs min ealda fæder   Ealhelm hāten,
wīs ealdorman,   woruldġesǣliġ.
Ne sceolon mē on þǣre þēode   þeġenas ætwītan        220
þæt iċ of ðisse fyrde   fēran wille,
eard ġesēcan   nū mīn ealdor liġeð
forhēawen æt hilde.   Mē is þæt hearma mǣst –
hē wæs ǣġ[ð]er mīn mǣġ   and mīn hlāford.»          224
Þā hē forð ēode;   fǣhðe ġemunde
þæt hē mid orde   ānne ġerǣhte
flotan on þām folċe   þæt sē on foldan læġ
forweġen mid his wǣpne.   Ongan þā winas manian     228
frȳnd and ġefēran   þæt hī forð ēodon.
Offa ġemǣlde,   æscholt āscēoc:
«Hwæt, þū, Ælfwine,   hafast ealle ġemanode
þeġenas tō þearfe.   Nū ūre þēoden līð,             232
eorl on eorðan,   ūs is eallum þearf
þæt ūre ǣġhwylċ   ōþerne bylde,
wigan tō wīġe,   þā hwīle þe hē wǣpen mæġe
habban and healdan,   heardne mēċe,                 236

34

Then there went forwards / proud thanes↑,
unafraid men, / they-hastened keenly:
they↑ wished then all↑ / [to do] one↓ of-two [things],
life↓ to-lay-down / or dear [friend↓] to-avenge.
So them↓ urged onward / son of-Æ.,
warrior in-years young, / in-words made-speech;
Æ. then talked, / he with valour spoke:
"Recall those times / when we often over mead talked,
when we on bench / vow↓ raised,
heroes↑ in hall, / about tough fighting.
Now [one] can discover / who (is) brave ( )!
I wish my descent↓ / to-all to-declare,
that I was among [the] Mercians / of-great family;
was my grand-father / E. called,
wise officer, / in-life-prospering.
Not need me↓ in that people / men↑ reproach
that I out-of this army / to-go wish,
[my] home↓ to-seek, / now my leader lies
cut-down in battle. / To-me is it of-griefs [the] greatest –
he was both my kinsman / & my lord."
Then he forward moved; / cause-of-hate recalled
so-that he with weapon-point / one↓ reached
sailor↓ in that horde, / so-that he on ground lay
borne-down by his weapon./He-began then companions↓ to-rally
friends↓ & comrades↓, / so-that they forward moved.
O. spoke, / ash-spear↓ he-shook:
"Yes, you, Æ., / have ( ) urged-on (all)
[the] thanes↓ at need. / Now our lord lies [dead],
earl on earth, / for-us (all) there-is ( ) need
that of-us each↑ / the-other↓ should-encourage,
warrior↓ to war, / for-the time that he weapon↓ can
retain & hold, / hard blade↓,

gār and gōd swurd. Ūs Godrīċ hæfð,
earh Oddan bearn, ealle beswiċene.
Wēnde þæs formoni man, þā hē on mēare rād,
on wlancan þām wicge, þæt wǣre hit ūre hlāford;    240
forþan wearð hēr on felda folc tōtwǣmed,
scyldburh tōbrocen – ābrēoðe his anġin
þæt hē hēr swā maniġne man āflȳmde!»
Lēofsunu ġemǣlde and his linde āhōf,    244
bord tō ġebeorge. Hē þām beorne oncwæð:
«Iċ þæt ġehāte þæt iċ heonon nelle
flēon fōtes trym, ac wille furðor gān,
wrecan on ġewinne mīnne winedrihten.    248
Ne þurfon mē embe Stūrmere stedefæste hǣlæð
wordum ætwītan, nū mīn wine ġecranc,
þæt iċ hlāfordlēas hām sīðie,
wende fram wīġe, ac mē sceal wǣpen niman,    252
ord and īren!» Hē ful yrre wōd,
feaht fæstlīċe – flēam hē forhogode!
Dunnere þā cwæð, daroð ācwehte,
unorne ċeorl, ofer eall clypode,    256
bæd þæt beorna ġehwylċ Byrhtnōð wrǣċe:
«Ne mæġ nā wandian sē þe wrecan þenċeð
frēan on folċe, nē for fēore murnan!»
þā hī forð ēodon, fēores hī ne rōhton.    260

## THE END

Ongunnon þā hīredmen heardlīċe feohtan,
grame gārberend, and God bǣdon
þæt hī mōston ġewrecan hyra winedrihten
and on hyra fēondum fyl ġewyrcan.    264
Him se ġȳsel ongan ġeornlīċe fylstan:
hē wæs on Norðhymbron heardes cynnes,

spear↓ & worthy sword↓. / Us↓ G.↑ has,
cowardly O.'s son, / all↓ betrayed.
Believed it↓ too-many [a] man, / when he on mare rode-off,
on (that) fine ( ) steed, / that (it) was ( ) our lord;
wherefore became here on [battle-]field / [the] army↑ divided,
shield-defence broken-up – / be-ruined his life,
that he here so many / [a] man led-to-flight!"
L. spoke / & his linden-[shield]↓ raised,
plank-[shield]↓ in defence; he to-the warrior said:
"I ( ) promise (this), / that I from-here will-not
flee [a] foot's space, / but will more-forward go,
avenge in battle / my kind-lord↓.
Not will-need me↓ around Sturmer / resolute people↑
in-words to-reproach, / now my friend has-fallen,
that I lord-less / home will-go,
will-turn from battle; / but me↓ must weapon↑ take,
point↑ & [=or] iron↑." / He very angry advanced,
fought determinedly – / flight↓ he scorned!
D. then spoke, / javelin↓ he-brandished,
[a] plain freeman, / to all he-called-out,
bade that soldiers' each↑ / B.↓ should-avenge:
"Not can not-at-all hesitate / he that to-avenge intends
[his] lord↓ on [the V.] army, / nor for [his] life worry!"
Then they forwards moved, / of-life they not took-heed.

## THE END

Began then [the] household-men / bravely to-fight,
fierce spear-bearers, / & God↓ petitioned
that they might avenge / their kind-lord
& upon their foes / destruction↓ work.
Them↓ the hostage began / keenly to-support:
he was among [the] Northumbrians / of-hardy kin,

Ecglāfes bearn.  Him wæs Æscferð nama;
hē ne wandode nā  æt þām wīgplegan                    268
ac hē fȳsde forð  flān ġenēhe;
hwīlon hē on bord scēat,  hwīlon beorn tæsde;
æfre embe stunde  hē sealde sume wunde
þā hwīle ðe hē wæpna  wealdan mōste.                  272
Þā ġȳt on orde stōd  Ēadweard se langa,
ġearo and ġeornful;  ġylpwordum spræċ
þæt hē nolde flēogan  fōtmæl landes,
ofer bæċ būgan,  þā his betera leġ.                   276
Hē bræċ þone bordweall  and wið þā beornas feaht
oð þæt hē his sinċġyfan  on þām sæmannum
wurðlīċe wreċ  ær hē on wæle lǣġe.
Swā dyde Æþerīċ,  æþele ġefēra,                       280
fūs and forðġeorn,  feaht eornoste,
Sībyrhtes brōðor,  and swīðe mæniġ ōþer.
Clufon ċellod bord –  cēne hī weredon!
Bærst bordes læriġ  and sēo byrne sang               284
gryrelēoða sum.  Þā æt gūðe slōh
Offa þone sǣlidan,  þæt hē on eorðan fēoll;
and ðǣr Gaddes mæġ  grund ġesōhte:
raðe wearð æt hilde  Offa forhēawen;                 288
hē hæfde ðēah ġeforþod  þæt hē his frēan ġehēt
swā hē bēotode ær  wið his bēahġifan
þæt hī sceoldon bēgen  on burh rīdan,
hāle tō hāme,  oððe on here crin[c]gan,              292
on wælstōwe  wundum sweltan;
hē læġ ðeġenlīċe  ðēodne ġehende.
Ðā wearð borda ġebræċ!  Brimmen wōdon,
gūðe ġegremode;  gār oft þurhwōd                     296
fæġes feorhhūs.  For[ð] ðā ēode Wīstān,
Þurstānes suna,  wið þās secgas feaht.

E.'s son, / his (name) was Æ. ( );
he not hesitated not-at-all / in the war-work
but he poured forth / arrows enough;
sometimes he into shield shot, / sometimes warrior↓ tore-into;
ever after-[a]-while [=again] / he delivered some wound
during-that time that he weapons↓ / wield might.
Then still in front-line stood / E. the tall,
ready & keen; / in-vaunt-words he-said
that he would-not flee / [a] foot-space of-land,
to [the] rear move, / when his superior lay [dead].
He broke-through the shield-wall / & with the men fought
until he his treasure-giver [B.↓] / on the seamen
worthily avenged / before he among [the] dead lay.
So-too did Æ. / [a] noble fellow-warrior,
keen & forward-pressing, / he-fought energetically,
S.'s brother↑, / & very many another [with him].
They-split ?whitened shield, / brave[ly] selves defended.
Burst shield's rim↑ / & the chain-mail sang
(one) of-[its]-terror-songs ( ). / Then in battle struck
O.↑ the seafarer↓, / so-that he to ground fell;
& there G.'s kinsman [O.?] / [also] the-ground↓ sought:
quickly was in fighting / O. cut-down;
he had though fulfilled / what he to-his lord promised,
as he vowed earlier / to his ring-giver [B.]
that they should both / into [the] town ride,
safe to [their] home, / or in [the] army perish,
on [the] slaughter-field / from-wounds die;
he lay nobly / (near) [his] lord ( ).
Then there-was shields' crashing! / [The] seamen advanced,
through-war enraged; / spear often transfixed
fated life-house [=body]. / Forth then went W.,
Th.'s son, / against these men fought.

Hē wæs on ġeþrang   hyra þrēora bana
ǣr him Wīġel[m]es bearn   on þām wæle lǣġe.   300
Þǣr wæs stīð ġemōt;   stōdon fæste
wigan on ġewinne.   Wīġend cruncon,
wundum wēriġe;   wæl fēol on eorþan.
Ōswold and Ēadwold   ealle hwīle   304
bēġen þā ġebrōþru   beornas trymedon;
hyra winemāgas   wordon bǣdon
þæt hī þǣr æt ðearfe   þolian sceoldon,
unwāclīċe   wǣpna nēotan.   308
Byrhtwold maþelode,   bord hafenode;
sē wæs eald ġenēat;   æsc ācwehte.
Hē ful baldlīċe   beornas lǣrde:
«Hiġe sceal þē heardra,   heorte þē cēnre,   312
mōd sceal þē māre   þe ūre mæġen lȳtlað.
Hēr līð ūre ealdor   eall forhēawen,
gōd on grēote:   ā mæġ gnornian
sē ðe nū fram þis wīġplegan   wendan þenċeð!   316
Iċ eom frōd fēores;   fram iċ ne wille,
ac iċ mē be healfe   mīnum hlāforde,
be swā lēofan men,   licgan þenċe.»
Swā hī Æþelgāres bearn   ealle bylde,   320
Godrīċ tō gūþe;   oft hē gār forlēt,
wælspere windan   on þā Wīċingas.
Swā hē on þām folċe   fyrmest ēode,
hēow and hȳnde   o[ð] þæt hē on hilde ġecranc.   324
Næs þæt nā se Godrīċ   þe ðā gū[ð]e forbēah! . . . .

He was in [the] mêlée / of-them of-three [the] killer
before ( )W.'s descendant [W.]/among the dead lay (himself).
There was stiff contest; / stood firm
[the] warriors in [the] struggle. / Fighters collapsed,
by-wounds worn-down; / [the] dead fell to [the] ground.
O. & E. / all [the] time,
both those brothers, / [the] men↓ exhorted;
their dear-cousins↓ / in-words told
that they there at need / endure must,
unweakly / weapons↓ apply.
Byrhtwold spoke, / shield↓ he-raised;
he was [an] old[er] retainer; / ash-[spear]↓ he-shook.
He very courageously / [the] men↓ instructed:
"Mind must [be] the resoluter, / heart the bolder,
courage must [be] the greater, / as our strength dwindles.
Here lies our leader / all cut-about,
good-man in [the] dirt: / ever may be-sorry
he↑ who now from this war-work / to-go-away is-minded.
I am experienced in-life: away I ( ) will (not) [go],
but I ( ) by [the] side / of-my lord,
by so dear [a] man, / to lay (myself↓) intend."
So them↓ Æ.'s son↑ / all↓ encouraged,
G.↑ to [the] fight; / often he javelin↓ sent,
death-spear↓ flying / into the Vikings.
So he in that army / foremost went,
hacked & cut-down [men↓] / until he in combat fell.
Not-was that not-at-all the G. / who the battle↓ abandoned! . . . .

CONVENTIONS
[extra or explanatory word]
(transposed word)
subject ↑ object ↓
B. = Byrhtnoth   V. = Viking

**Verse Translation**

## PREPARATIONS

...broken was.
He called on each **hero   horse** let free,
**far** drive it   and **forward** step,
think on **hand's** power   and **heart**-courage.                4
When **Offa's** son   **once** saw
that the **earl** would tolerate   no lack of **effort**,
he re**leased** from his wrist   be**loved** hawk
to **fly** to the **forest**   and to the **fight** moved forward        8
that all should **understand**   that this was a **youth**
wouldn't **weaken** in **war**   when he took up **weapons.**
Like him, **Eadriċ** wanted   to serve his **elder,**
his lord, in the **fight;   forward** he carried              12
his **spear** to battle;   he had **special** thanks
so long his **hands   held** on to
**board**-shield, **broad** sword;   that **boast** he made good
when in **front** of his lord   he came to **fight.**            16
Then **Byrhtnoth** set   to sort his **battle**-groups:
he **rode round,**   showed the **recruits**
how to be **placed**   and hold **position,**
and their **round**-shields   hold **right,**                20
**firm** in **fist**;   to feel no **fear.**
When all the **people**   were **properly** stationed,
then he **alighted**   where he most **longed** to be,
with his own **house**-troops   he knew **wholly** loyal.         24

## THE CHALLENGES

Then on shore **stood, strongly** called out,
the **Vikings'** herald, with **voice** hailed them,
**eagerly, urged** the **ocean**-goers'
**embassy** to the **earl** where he stood **opposite:**         28
«Brave **seamen sent** me to you
told me to **say** you should **send** quickly
**silver** for **safety** and it'd be **sensible** for you
to buy off **trouble** with **tribute**             32
than have us, **harshly,** deal out **havoc.**
We needn't be **reduced** to war if you're **rich** enough:
we for **gold** will **give** you our **guarantee.**
If you **approve,** who are the most **important** here,     36
to **pay** and save your **people**
then give us **seamen,** on our own **assessment,**
**treasure** for a **truce,** accept our **treaty.**
With the **silver** we'll board **ship,**               40
**embark** on the sea, keep to our **bargain.**»
Then **Byrhtnoth** spoke, **board**-shield raised,
shook **slender spear,** gave **speech;**
**roused, resolute,** made his **reply:**            44
«Can you hear, **seamen,** what we **say** on our **side?**
Indeed we've **something** to **send** you – **spears,**
**deadly dart** and **durable** swords,
these make the **war**-tax you are **welcome** to collect!    48
**Messenger** of the sea**men, make** your way back,
tell your **people** a less **palatable** tale,
that here stands **uncowed** the **earl** with his **army**
who will **keep** this **country** safe,            52
Æthelred's **land,** my **liege's**
**folk** and **fields.** To **fall** is for

**heathens** in battle! It would be **humiliating** for you
to be off with our **shillings** to your **ships** 56
without a **fight** now so **far**
you've made an **entry into** our country!
You should not so **easily earn** our money
but **spear** and **sword** will **settle** it first, 60
**tough** combat, before we yield **tribute!**»

## AT THE FORD

He told his men to ready **shields,** gave his **soldiers** the advance
till along the **water**-front **everywhere** they stood.
Yet for the **sea**-channel the one **side** couldn't get at the other 64
for there came **flowing** in the **flood**-tide after the ebb,
and the **loop**-currents **locked** together. Too **long** it seemed
till when in **war** they could join **weapons.**
There the **Pant**-channel they **powerfully** lined, 68
the **Essex array** and the **ash**-boat-force,
not **either** could damage the **other**
except who by arrow-**flight** met his **fate.**
The **sea**-tide **subsided;** the **seamen** stood ready, 72
so many **Vikings** keen to ad**vance.**
Then as leader, **Byrhtnoth,** to hold the **bridge**
picked a tried **warrior, Wulfstan** his name,
**courageous** like all his **kin –** he was **Ceola's** son – 76
he brought down the **leading** man with a **lance**
who first **boldly** on the **bridgeway** ventured.
With **Wulfstan** stood two valiant **warriors,**
Ælfere and **Maccus,** a **mighty** pair, 80
they would not at the **ford** turn to **flight**
but **fiercely** they held out against the **foes**
while they could still **wield weapons.**
When they per**ceived,** clearly **saw** 84

that here they'd encountered **brave   bridge**-keepers,
then the con**temptible** enemy   began to **try** their **tricks,**
**urging** they be **offered**   a way **over,**
to cross the **ford,**   bring their **foot**-troops through.   88
Then the **earl**   from **over**-confidence
gave too much **room**   to that **ruthless** band of men.
He **called** out   over the **cold** water,
this son of **Byrhthelm**   (while the **boatmen** listened):   92
«There's **space** for you now,   **straight**-away
come to **grips** with us –   **God** himself alone
knows who'll hold **sway**   over this field of **struggle**.»

## THE BATTLE STARTS

Then the blood-**wolves waded** through,   not heeding **water,**   96
the Viking **war**-horde,   **west** over the Pant
through the **shining** wet   brought their **shields,**
carried to **land**   the **linden**-wood.
There set a**gainst** them,   **geared,** stood   100
**Byrhtnoth** and his men;   with their **board**-shields
he had them make a **war-wall,**   told his **warriors** stand
**fast** with the **foe.**   The **fight** was near,
and glory in **combat,**   the oc**casion** come   104
when **fated** men   must **fall** in battle.
A grim **row** was **raised**   as **ravens** wheeled,
and the **eagle** – **eager** for meat –   and on **earth** the **uproar!**
Then men sent from their **hands   hard** spears,   108
**sharp**-pointed   the **shafts** flew.
**Bows** were **busy,   board** took sword.
**Wild** was the **war**-surge,   **warriors** fell,
on both **sides   soldiers** dying.   112
**Wulfmær** was **wounded,**   came to that **wakeless** sleep,
(a kinsman of **Byrhtnoth**)   by sword-**blades**

(his own **sister's son**)   he was **savagely** cut down.
Yet on the **Vikings**   some **revenge** was **visited**.                    116
**Edward,** as I heard,   slew **one** of them
**straight** off with his **sword,**   didn't **spare** the **stroke**
that right at his **feet fell**   the **fated** warrior.
For this his **commander   congratulated** him,                    120
this his **chamberlain,**   when he had **chance** to.
So **steady**-resolved   they **stood** firm,
men in **battle,**   am**bitioned** keenly
theirs to be the **weapon**   to **win**                    124
**first** the life   of some **fated** man,
some **warrior** by their arms.   And the **wounded** fell.
The **sturdy** men **stood** their ground;   Byrhtnoth in**stilled** courage,
told them each **fighter**   should **fix** his mind on combat                    128
if he'd prove his **valour**   on the **Vikings.**

## BYRHTNOTH FIGHTS AND DIES

Then **went** the Veteran,   raised his **weapon**
and his **shield** as a **safety,**   attacked some **soldier.**
Bravely **advanced**   the **earl** on the churl.                    132
**Each** of the **other**   thought **ill** enough!
The **seaman sent** off   a **south**-made **spear**
so the **warriors'** lord   was **wounded.**
But he **shoved** with his **shield**   till the **shaft** broke                    136
and banged at the **spear**   till it **sprang** away.
**Angered** was the **earl:**   with his **own** spear he struck
the **insolent** Viking   who'd done him **injury.**
**Accurate** was his **aim.**   The **aged** leader sent the shaft                    140
clean through the **wretch's** throat,   **wrist** so guided it
as to snatch the **life**   of his **luckless** assailant.
Then a **second**   he **speedily shot** at,
**burst** some man's armour,   wounded him in the **breast**                    144

46

through the **hard** rings of mail:   in the **heart** lodged
the deadly spear-**end.**   The **earl** was the happier!
He laughed, **mighty** and brave,   gave his **Maker** thanks
for the **day's** work   the **Deity** had given.                          148
Then some Viking **launched**   a **light**-spear from hand,
**winging** it from his wrist;   only too **well** it flew,
into **Byrhtnoth's   body.**
Be**side** him **stood**   a young **soldier,**                          152
a youth in the **conflict,**   who full of **courage**
drew from the **body's** wound   the **bloody** spear.
He was **Wulfstan's** son,   young **Wulfmær;**
he sent the **hard** tip   **hurtling** back again;                       156
**dart's** point went in   so in the **dirt** lay
the **man** who so **murderously**   had attacked his **master.**
Some **enemy** in **armour**   then **approached** the **earl,**
wanted to **loot** him   as he **lay,** of                              160
**raiment** and **rings**   and **rich**-worked sword.
But **Byrhtnoth** drew   **brand** from sheath,
**grand, gleaming,**   and struck at the **aggressor.**
But swiftly inter**vened**   one of the **Vikings**                       164
and **shattered** the earl's   **shoulder.**
The **golden**-hilt sword   to the **ground tumbled,**
no way could he **hold** on   to the **hard-heavy** blade,
**wield** his **weapon** more.   Yet some **words** he managed,           168
grey-**haired** and battle-glorious,   put **heart** in his men,
told his **good friends**   always to **go forward.**
He no longer could stand **firm**   on his **feet**
but looked to **heaven high** above   and as a **hero** spoke:            172
«Receive my **gratitude,   God** of all,
for every **luckful** honour   I've enjoyed in **life.**
Yet now, **merciful Maker,**   I have the **most** need
that You should give as**sistance**   to my **soul**                      176

47

that my **spirit**   may **speed** to Thee,
come to Thy **kingdom,   King** of Angels,
**pass** through in **peace.** I **pray** You
that no **hell-demons**   may ever **hurt, defile** it.» 180
Then the **heathens   hacked** at him
and **both** the **bold** men   who **by** him stood,
**Ælfnoth** and Wulmær,   till they **also** died,
**lost** their **lives**   at their **lord's** side. 184

## GODRIC'S FLIGHT

Then they ran from the **battle**   who had no wish to **be** there:
and **Odda's** son   was **earliest** to leave;
he was called **Godriċ,**   he abandoned his **good** master
who'd often given him **many**   a fine **mare:** 188
now he leapt on that very **steed**   his lord had **sat** on,
used those **trappings**   he had no **title** to;
and his **brothers** with him   **both** rode off,
**Godwine & Godwiġ** –   they had little re**gard** for fighting 192
but turned from the **war-**strife,   made for the **woods,**
fled for **refuge,**   saved their **wretched** lives,
and with them more **people**   than was in any way **proper**
if they'd at all re**called**   the many **kindnesses,** 196
all the **help**   the **hero** had given them.
Just as much **Offa** had said   **earlier** on
at the **moot-**place   when there was a **meeting,**
that **many** spoke there   very **man**fully, 200
who when there was **need**   would **never** match their words.

## THE STAND

So was **lost**   the army's **leader,**
**Æthelred's earl.** They **all** saw,
his **hearth-**men,   that their **high-**lord was dead. 204

48

Yet still advanced   these **valiant** men;
**fearless** warriors,   they moved **forward** readily;
they **all** wanted   **one** of two things,
to avenge their **lord**   or **lay** down their **lives.**                  208
So the son of Ælfriċ   **urged** them on,
a **warrior** still young,   formed these **words;**
Ælfwine he was called –   spoke with **intensity.**
«I remember those **times**   we **talked** over our mead –          212
there on the **benches**   we made our **boasts,**
**heroes** in the **hall,**   about **hard** fighting:
now we can dis**cover**   who really has **courage.**
I would like to tell **all** of you   my **ancestry:**                     216
among the **Mercians**   I was of a **mighty** family:
**Ealhelm** was my grandfather,   the **alderman,**
**wise,**   of rank in this **world.**
No **person** shall re**proach** me –   no one of my **people** –     220
that I wanted to get **out,**   leave this **army,**
and make for **home**   now my **high**-lord lies
**cut** down in the **conflict.**   For me it's the **cruellest** of blows –
he was both **kinsman**   and **commander.**»                          224
So he went **forward,**   **fuelled** by his **feud,**
till with his **sword**   he brought down one **soldier**
of the **enemy** force –   who lay dead on the **earth**
**felled** by his weapon.   He urged on his **friends,**                  228
his comrades in **arms**   that they should go **onwards.**
**Offa** spoke,   brandished **ash**-spear:
«Yes, Ælfwine,   you have **encouraged** us **all**
when we **needed** it.   Now our **noble** lord lies dead,              232
the **earl** on the **earth,**   we **all** must,
**each** of us, **exhort**   the **other,**
as **warriors** to **war,**   so long as **weapon**
we **have** and **hold,**   **hard** blade,                              236

49

spear and **good** sword. **Godrič,**
the coward son of **Odda,** has betrayed us **all:**
**most men** thought, when he rode off on that **mare,**
that **well**-known mount, that it **was** our leader,                   240
and so on the **field** our **folk** were confused,
the **shield**-wall **shattered. Shame** on his deeds
that he **made** so **many** a **man** flee!»
**Leofsunu** spoke, raised his **linden**-shield                   244
in de**fence,** responded to his **fellow-fighter:**
«I **swear** this, I will not **step** back
a **foot**'s space! Rather I'll go **further** ahead,
avenge in **battle** my **benefactor.**                   248
No one round **Sturmer,** steady in judgment,
will ever need ac**cuse** me, now my **kind** lord's fallen,
of **making** for home, deserting my **master,**
running from **war:** better a **weapon** take me,                   252
**point** or blade.» Then in a **passion**
he **fought fiercely, flight** he scorned.
Next **Dunnere** spoke: **dart**-spear he shook,
frank as **commoner** he **called** out to all,                   256
told them their **blows** would be for **Byrhtnoth:**
«He must not **hesitate** who **hopes** to avenge
our **lord** on the foe, nor heed his own **life.**»
So they went **onward,** heedless of their **own** safety.                   260

## THE END

The **household** troops fought **hard,**
**grim** spear-wielders, to **God** they prayed
to be allowed to a**venge** their re**vered** lord
and to bring **death** to his **destroyers.**                   264
A **hostage** with them **helped whole**-heartedly.
He was from **Northumbria,** of kin re**nowned** for fighting.

**Ashferth** was his name,  **Ecglaf's** son.
He did not hold **back**  in the **battle**-play                    268
but **issued** a stream  of **arrows;**
sometimes he hit the **shield,**  sometimes the **soldier**
but again and ag**ain**  he wounded m**en**
all the **while** he still **wielded  weapon.**                    272
**Out** in front  stood **Edward** the tall,
**ready** and **resourceful;**  he spoke his **resolve**
that he would not **flee**  a **foot**-space of land,
**turn** in r**etreat,**  now his lord had been **taken.**         276
He broke through the **van**  and fought the **Vikings**
until on those **raiders**  he'd avenged **aright**
his **lord**  and himself **lay lifeless.**
So too did **Ætheriĉ,  excellent** man,                            280
**eager** and **able**  he fought **urgently** –
he was **Sibyrht's** brother –  and **so** too many others did.
They shattered **blanked** shields,  **boldly** defended themselves.
**Shield**-rim **snapped**  and chain-mail **sang** out            284
its **gruesome** hymn.  There in the **grim** fighting
**Offa** struck some **seaman**  so he **sank** to the **earth**
but there too **Gadd's** son  in turn hit the **ground.**
**Quickly** in the **conflict**  Offa was **cut** down;             288
yet he had ac**complished**  what he told his **commander**
when earlier he **promised**  to his **provider**
that the **two** of them  would ride back to **town,**
come **home whole**  or perish as one in the **heat** of battle,   292
die of their **wounds**  on the field of **war.**
Now he **lay** in all **loyalty**  close to his **lord.**
There was the **shatter** of **shields.**  The **seamen** came on,
raging in **war.  Weapon** often transfixed                        296
some **fated** body.  **Forward** then came Wistan,
**Thurstan's son,  tackled** the seamen.

In the **throng** of battle   he killed **three** of them
before **Wiġelm's** descendent   lay also over**whelmed.**      300
This was **fierce** confrontation:   **firm** stood
the **warriors** in the **whirl** of battle.   **War**-men fell,
on the ground, **cut**-weary   **collapsed** lifeless
**Oswald** and **Eadwold**   **all** this time,      304
**brothers,**   encouraged the **battlers,**
told their **friends**   this **phrase**
that now when it **mattered most**   they must **make** the effort,
un**sparingly**   use their **swords.**      308
**Byrhtwold** spoke,   raised **board**-shield;
he was an **older** warrior;   he brandished **ash**-spear
and full of **courage**   addressed his **comrades.**
«Minds must be the firm**er,**   hearts the bold**er,**      312
**soul's strength** the greater,   as our re**sources** lessen.
Here **lies** our **lord,   lethally** wounded,
**good** man on the **ground.**   May he **grieve** for ever
who from this **war-work**   would consider **withdrawing.**      316
I am **old** in **age,   away** I won't,
but **myself**   by my **master,**
by so be**loved** a man,   would finally **lie.** »
Then **Æthelgar's** son   **encouraged** them all,      320
Godriċ, in the **fight.**   He let **fly** a spear
to **speed** its deadly way   into the **seamen's** ranks;
so he went **first**   among that **folk,**
**cut** and **killed**   until he too in the **conflict** fell.      324
That was not the **Godriċ**   who fled the en**gagement!** . . . .

# SOURCE TEXT

*The Bodleian transcript in Rawlinson B.203 ff.7–12*
*of Cotton Otho A.Xii.3.f.57*[1]

..... bꞃocen ƿuꞃðe. het þa hyꞃꞃa hƿæne. hoꞃſ
foꞃ lætan feoꞃ afysan ⁊ foꞃð gangan hicgan to handum ⁊ t hige goðū. þ þ offan mæȝ    4
æꞃeſt onꝼunde þ ſe eoꞃl nolde yꞃhðo ge-
þolian he let him þa oꝼ handon leoꝼne
fleogan haꝼoc ƿið þæſ holteſ ⁊ to þæꞃe    8
hilde ſtop. be þā man mihte oncnaƿan
þ se cniht nolde ƿacian æt þā ƿ....ge þa
he to ƿæƿnū feng. eac hi ƿolde eaðꞃic
hiſ ealdꞃe ge læſtan fꞃean to gefeohte    12
on gan þa foꞃð beꞃan gaꞃ to guþe he
hæfðe god geþanc þa hƿile þe he mið handum healdan mihte boꞃð ⁊ bꞃad ſƿuꞃð
beot he gelæſte þa he ætfoꞃan hiſ fꞃean    16
feohtan sceolde.

Ða þæꞃ byꞃhtnoð ongan beoꞃnaſ tꞃy-
mian. ꞃad ⁊ ꞃædde ꞃincū tæhte hu
hi ſceoldon ſtandan ⁊ þone ſtede healdan ⁊ bæd þ hyꞃa ꞃandan ꞃihte heol-    20
don fæſte mið folman ⁊ ne foꞃhtedon-

---

[1] The numbers given against the Source Text correspond to the line numbers of the Edited Text

na. þa he hæfðe þ folc fægere ge trymeð
he lihte þa mið leoðon þær hi leofoft
pær. þær he his heorð peroð holðoft piste.    24
þa ftoð onftæðe ftiðlice clÿpoðe picinga-
ár porðū mælðe. fe on beot abeað bri liþen-
ðra æ rænðe to þam eorle. þær he on ofre-    28
ftoð. me renðon to þe. ræmenfnelle hetonðe
recgan þ þu moft renðan raðe beagaf pið
ge beorge. 7 eop betere if. þ ge þif ne garrær    32
mið garole forgÿlðon. þon pe fpa hearðe
..ulðe dælon. ne þurfe pe us rpillan. gif ge
fpeðaþ to þā. pe pillað pið þā golðe grið
fæftnian. gÿf þu þat ge ræðest þe her ri-    36
coft eart. þ þu þine leoða lÿran pille. rÿl-
lan ræmannū on hÿra sÿlfra ðō. feoh
pið freoðe. 7 niman frið æt us. pepillaþ    40
mið þam fceattū. uf to fcÿpe gangan. on
flot feran. 7 eop friþes healðan; Bÿrht-
noð ma þe loðe borð harenoðe. panð pacne
æsc. porðū mælðe. ÿrre 7 anræð ageaf hi    44
anðfpare. gehÿrft þu fæliða hpæt þif
folc segeð. hi pillað eop togarole garar
sÿllan æt trÿnneorð 7 ealðe fpurð. þa
heregeatu þe eop æt hilðe ne ðeah. bri    48
manna boða abeoð eft ongean sege þi-
nū leoðū miccle laþre spell þ her ftÿnt
unforcuð eorl mið hif peroðe þe pile ge-    52
algean eþel þÿrne æþelreðes earð eal-
ðres mines folc 7 folðan feallan sceo-

lon hæþene æt hilðe to heanlic me þin-
ceð þ ʒe mið uнū ſceattū to scÿpe                    56
ʒanʒon unbe fohtene nuʒe þus feoн hi-
ðeн on uнne eaнð inbecomon ne sceole
ʒe ſpa softe нinc ʒe ʒanʒan uſ sceal oнð        60
⁊ ecʒ æнʒe нemanʒнí ʒuð pleʒa æнþe
ʒofol нÿllon.
   Het þa boнð beнan beoнnas ʒanʒan þ
hi on þā eá ſteðe ealle stoðon ne mihte            64
þæнfoн пæteнe peнoð to þā oðнum þæн
com flopenðe floð æfteн ebban lucon
laʒu ſtнeamas to lanʒ hit him þuhte
hpænne hi to ʒæðeнe ʒaнas beнon
   Hi þæн panтan ſtнeam mið пнaſſe        68
be ſtoðon eaſtнeaxena oнð ⁊ ſe æsc heнe
ne mihte hÿнa æniʒoþнū ðeнian buтon
hнa þuнh flaneſ flÿht fÿlʒename: Se
floð uт ʒe paт þa floтan ſtoðon ʒeaнope    72
picinʒa fela нiʒes ʒeoнne. Het þa hæleða hleo healdan þa bнicʒe нiʒan нiʒ-
heaнðne ſe пæſ haтen pulfſтan caſ-
ne mið hiſ cÿnne þ пæſ ceolan нunu        76
þe ðone foнman man mið hiſ fнancā
of sceaт þe þæн baldlicoſt on þa
bнicʒe ſтop. þæн ſтoðon mið pulfſтāe
нiʒan unfoнhte. ælfeнe ⁊ maccus mo-        80
ðiʒe тpeʒen þa noldon æт þā foнða
fleā ʒe pÿнcan. ac hi fæſтlice piðða fÿnð
peнedon þa hpile þe hi pæpna pealdan

moſton. þa hi þ onᵹeaton ⁊ ᵹeoꝛneᵹe   84
ꝼapon. þ hi þæꝛ bꝛicᵹ peaꝛðas biteꝛe
ꝼundon. onᵹunnon lyteᵹian þa laðe
ᵹyſtaꝛ. bædon þ hi upᵹanᵹan aᵹan
moſton. oꝼeꝛ þone ꝼoꝛð ꝼaꝛan ꝼeþan   88
lædan. Đa ꞃe eoꝛl onᵹan ꝼoꝛ hiꞅ o-
ꝼeꝛmoðe alyꝼan landeꞅ to ꝼela la þeꝛe
ðeoðe onᵹan ceallian þa oꝼeꝛcalð pæteꝛ byꝛhtelmeꞅ beaꝛn beoꝛnaꞅ ᵹeh-   92
lyꞅton nu eop iꞅ ᵹeꝛymeð ᵹað ꝛicene
to uꞅ ᵹuman to ᵹuþe ᵹoð ana pat hꝛa
þæꝛe pæl ꞅtope pealdan mote. Woðon   96
þa pæl pulꝼaꞅ ꝼoꝛ pæteꝛe ne muꝛnon
picinᵹa peꝛoð peꞅt oꝼeꝛ pantan oꝼeꝛ
ꞅciꝛ pæteꝛ scylðaꞅ peᵹon liðmen to
lande linðe bæꝛon þæꝛ onᵹean ᵹꝛamū   100
ᵹeaꝛope ꞅtodon. Byꝛhtnoð mið beoꝛ-
num he mið boꝛðū het pyꝛcan þone
pi haᵹan. ⁊ þ peꝛoð healdan ꝼæꞅte. pið
ꝼeonðū. þa pæꞅ ꝼohte nehtiꝛ æt ᵹe   104
tohte pæꞅ ꞅeo tið cumen þ þæꝛ ꝼæᵹe
men ꝼeallan ꞅceolðon þæꝛ peaꝛð hꝛe-
am a haꝼen hꝛemmas pundon. eaꝛn æses
ᵹeoꝛn. pæꞅ on eoꝛþan cyꝛm. Hi leton þa oꝼ   108
ꝼolman ꝼeol heaꝛðe ſpeꝛu. ᵹe ᵹꝛunðe ne ᵹa-
ꝛas ꝼleoᵹan. boᵹan pæꝛon bysiᵹe. boꝛðoꝛð
onꝼenᵹ. biteꝛ pæs se beaðuꝛæs. beoꝛnaꞅ
ꝼeollon. onᵹe hpæðeꝛe hanð hyꝛꞅaꞅ laᵹon.   112
Wunð peaꝛð pulꝼmæꝛ. pæl ꝛæꞅte ᵹe ceaꞅ.

byꞃhtnoðes mæȝ he miðbillū peaꞃð
hiſ ſpuſꞇeꞃ sunuspiðe foꞃ heapen. þæꞃ
pæꞃð piciŋū piþeꞃlean aȝyꝼen. ȝe hyꞃðe 116
ic þ eaðpeaꞃð anne sloȝe. ꞃpiðe mið his
ſpuꞃðe. spenȝeſ ne pyꞃnðe. þ him æꞇ foꞇū
ꝼeoll ꝼæȝe cempa. þæſ him hiſ ðeoðen 120
þanc ȝe ꞃæðe. þā buꞃþene þa he byꞃe hæꝼðe.
Spa ſꞇemneꞇꞇonsꞇið hicȝenðe hyꞃas æꞇ
hilðe hoȝoðon ȝeoꞃne hpa þæꞃ mið oꞃðe 124
æꞃoſꞇ mihꞇe on ꝼæȝean menꝼeoꞃh ȝe
pinnan. piȝan mið pæꞃnū. pælꝼeol on
eoꞃðan. ſꞇoðon ſꞇæðe ꝼæſꞇe. Sꞇihꞇe hi
byꞃhtnoð bæð þ hyꞃꞃa ȝe hpylc hoȝoðe 128
to piȝe. þe on ðenon polðe ðom ȝe ꝼeohꞇan.
  Woð þa piȝes heaꞃð. pæꞃen up á hoꝼ boꞃð
to ȝebeoꞃȝe ⁊ pið þæꞃ beoꞃneſ ſꞇop. eoðe
ſpa anꞃæð. eoꞃl to þā ceoꞃle. æȝþeꞃ hyꞃa 132
oðꞃū. yꝼeles hoȝoðe. ſenðe ðaꞃe sæꞃinc.
suþeꞃne ȝaꞃ. þ ȝepunðoð peaꞃð piȝena
hlaꝼoꞃð. he sceaꝼ þa mið ðā scylðe. þæꞇ 136
ſe ſceaꝼꞇ to bæꞃſꞇ. ⁊ þ ſpeꞃe ſpꞃenȝðe.
þ hiꞇ ſpꞃanȝ onȝean. ȝeȝꞃe moð peaꞃð
se ȝuðꞃinc. he mið ȝaꞃe ſꞇanȝ. plancne
piciŋ. þe hi þa punðe foꞃȝeaꝼ. ꝼꞃoð
pæꞃ se ꝼyꞃð ꞃinc. he leꞇ hiſ ꝼꞃancan 140
paðan. þuꞃh ðæꞃ hyꞃses halſ hanð pisoðe
þ he on þā ꝼæꞃ sceaðan ꝼeoꞃhȝe ꞃæhꞇe.
Ða he oþeꞃne oꝼsꞇlice sceaꞇ þ seo byꞃne 144
to bæꞃſꞇ. he pæſ on bꞃeoſꞇū punð. þuꞃh

ða hrinȝlocā hí æt heortan stoð æt-
terneorð. ſe eorl þær þe bliþra. Hloh þa
moðiman. ſæðe me to ðe þanc. ðæs dæȝ  148
ƿeorces þe hí ðrihten forȝeaf. Forlet
þa ðrenȝa rū ðaroð of handa fleoȝan
of folman. þ se to forð ȝe ƿat þurh
ðone æþelan æþelreðes þeȝen. Him be
healfe ſtoð hyſe ún ƿeaxen cniht on  152
ȝe campe. ſe full carlice bræð of þam
beorne. bloðiȝne ȝar ƿulfſtaneſ bearn.
ƿulfmær ſe ȝeonȝa forlet for heardne  156
faran eft onȝean orð in ȝe ƿoð þ se on
eorþan læȝ þe his þeoden ær þearle
ȝeræhte. eode þa ȝesyrpeð secȝ to þam
eorle he ƿolðe þær beorneſ beaȝaſ ȝe-  160
fecȝan reaf ⁊ hrinȝaſ ⁊ ȝere noð
ſƿurð.
Þa byrhtnoð bræð bill of sceðe brað
⁊ brun eccȝ. ⁊ on þa byrnan ſloh to
raþe hine ȝelette liðmanna ſum. þa he  164
þær eorles earm amyrðe feoll þa to
folðan fealohilte ſƿurð ne mihte he
ȝehealðan heardne mece ƿæþneſ ƿealð-  168
ðan. þa ȝyt þ ƿorð ȝe cƿæð harhilðerinc
hyſſaſ bylðe bæð ȝanȝan forð ȝode ȝe
feran. ne mihte þa on fotū lenȝ fæſte
ȝe ſtunðan. He to heofenū ƿlat ȝe  172
þance þe ðeoða ƿalðenð ealra þæra
ƿynna þe ic on ƿorulðe ȝe bað. Nu ic

ah milðe metoð mæste þearfe. ꝥ þu
minū ʒaſte ʒodes ʒeunne. ꝥ min ſapul    176
to ðe siðian mote on þin ʒe pealð þeoðen enʒla mið friþe ferian. ic eom
frymði to þe ꝥ hi helsceaðan hynan    180
ne moton; Ða hine heofon hæðene
scealcaſ. ⁊ beʒen þa beornas þe hi biʒ-
ſtodon. ælfnoð ⁊ pulmær beʒen laʒonða
onemn hyra frean feorh ʒe sealðon. Hi    184
buʒon þa fram beaðupe þe þær beon nolðon þær purðon oððan beorn. ærest
on fleame ʒodric fram ʒuþe ⁊ þone
ʒodan forlet þe hi mæniʒne oft mear    188
ʒe ſealðe he ʒe hleop þone eoh þe ahte
hiſ hlaforð on þā ʒe ræðū þe hit riht
ne pæſ ⁊ hiſ broðru mið him beʒen
ærðon ʒodrine ⁊ ʒodriʒ ʒu þe ne ʒymðon    192
ac pendon frā þā piʒe ⁊ þone puðu
sohton fluʒon on ꝥ fæsten ⁊ hyra feo-
reburʒon ⁊ manna ma þoñ hit æniʒ
mæð pære ʒyf hi þa ʒe earnunʒa ealle    196
ʒe munðon þe he him to ðuʒuþe ʒeðon
hæfðe spa hi offa on ðæʒ ær aſæðe
on þā meþel ſteðe þa he ʒe mot hæfðe ꝥ þær moðelice maneʒa ſrræcon    200
þe eft æt þære þolian nolðon.
Þa pearð afeallen þær folces ealðor æ-
þelpeðes eorl ealle ʒe ſapon heorð ʒe-
neatas ꝥ hyra heorra læʒ. þa ðær pen-    204

ðon forð plance þeȝenaſ un earȝe men
efſton ȝeorne. hi poldon þa ealle oðer
tpeȝa liſ for lætun oððe leoſne ȝe ppe-    208
can. Spa hi bylde forð beapn ælfnicer
piȝa pintrum ȝeonȝ porðū mælðe.
ælfpine þa cpæð he on ellen ſppæc ȝe
munu þa mæla þe pe oſt æt meoðo    212
ſppæcon þoñ pe on bence beot aho-
ſon hæleð on healle ȳm be heapð ȝe
pinn. Nu mæȝ cunnian hpa cene sȳ
ic pylle mine æþelo eallū ȝe cȳþan.    216
Þ ic pæſ on myrcon miccles cȳnnes
pæs min ealda ſæðer ealhelm haten
pis ealðorman poruld ȝe ſæliȝ. ne
sceolon me on þæpe þeoðe þeȝenaſ æt    220
pitan. Þ ic oſ ðiſſe fȳnðe feran pille
earðȝe ſe can nu min ealðor liȝeð for
heapen æt hilðe me iſ Þ heapma mæſt.
he pæſ æȝðer min mæȝ ⁊ min hlaforð.    224
þa he forð eoðe. ſæhðe ȝemunðe Þ he mið
orðe anne ȝepæhte. flotan on þā folce
Þ se on folðan læȝ for peȝen mið hiſ    228
pæpne. onȝan þa pinaſ manian fpȳnð
⁊ ȝe feran Þ hi forð eoðon. offa ȝe
mælðe. æsc holt aſceoc. hpæt þu ælfpine
haſaſt ealle ȝemanoðe. þeȝenaſ to þe-    232
apſe nu upe þeoðen lið. eorl on eorðā
uſ iſ eallū þearſ Þ upe æȝhpylc oþer-
ne bylde piȝan to piȝe þa hpile þe he

ƿæpen mæȝe habban ⁊ healdan heaɲ- 236
dne mece. ȝaɲ ⁊ ȝod ſpuɲd. us ȝodɲic
hæfð eaɲh oððan beaɲn ealle be ſpi-
cene. þende þæſ foɲ moniman þa he
on meaɲe ɲad on plancan þā picȝe. 240
þ ƿæɲe hit uɲe hlafoɲd. foɲ þan peaɲð
heɲ on felda folc to tɲæmed scÿld buɲh
to bɲocen abɲeoðe hiſ anȝin. þ he heɲ
ſɲa maniȝne man aflÿmde. leof ſunu 244
ȝe mælde ⁊ hiſ linde a hof boɲd to ȝe
beoɲȝe. he þā beoɲne on cpæð. Ic þ ȝe-
hate þ ic heonon nelle fleon fotes
tɲÿm ac pille fuɲðoɲȝan. ppecan on 248
ȝe pinne minne pine dɲihten. ne þuɲ-
fon me embeſtuɲmeɲe stede fæste hæ-
læð. poɲðū æt pitan. nu min pine ȝe-
cɲanc þ ic hlafoɲdleas hā sidie þende 252
fɲā piȝe ac me ſceal ƿæpen niman.
oɲð ⁊ iɲen he ful ÿppe pod. feaht fæst-
lice fleam he foɲhoȝode. ðunneɲe þa
cpæð daɲoð a cpehte un oɲne ceoɲl o- 256
feɲ eall clÿpode. bæd þ beoɲna ȝe hpÿlc
bÿɲhtnoð ppece. ne mæȝ na pandian
se þe ppecan þenceð fɲean on folce
ne foɲ feoɲe muɲnan. þa hi foɲð eo- 260
don feoɲes hineɲohton onȝunnon þa
hiɲed men heaɲdlice feohtan. ȝɲame
ȝaɲbeɲend ⁊ ȝod bædon þæt hi moſton ȝeppecan hÿɲa pine dɲihten. ⁊ 264

on hyra feondū fyl geþyrcan. him  
se gyrel ongan geornlice fylstan. he  
þær on norð hymbron heardes cynnes  
ecglafes bearn him þær æscferð nama.  
he ne wandode na æt þā wig plegan. ac he     268  
fysde forð flan genehe. hwilon he on bord  
sceat hwilon beorn tæsde æfne embe stunde  
he sealde sume wunde. þa hwile ðe he wæp-     272  
na wealdan moste.  
Þa gyt on orðe stod eadweard se langa  
gearo ⁊ geornful. gylpwordū spræc þ  
he nolde fleogan fotmællandes. ofer bæc     276  
bugan þa his betera leg. he bræc þone  
bord weall ⁊ wið þa beornas feaht oð þ  
he his sincgyfan on þā sæmannū wurð-  
lice wrec ær he on wæle lege. Swa dyðe  
æþeric æþele gefera fus ⁊ forð georn     280  
feaht eornoste sibyrhtes broðor ⁊  
swiðe mænig oþer clufon cellod bord  
cene hi weredon bærst bordes lærig ⁊     284  
seo byrne sang gryre leoða sū. þa æt  
guðe sloh offa þone sælidan þ he on  
eorðan feoll. ⁊ ðær gaddes mæg grund  
gesohte. raðe weard æt hilde offa for     288  
heawen he hæfde ðeah geforþod þ he his  
frean gehet swa he beotode ær wið his  
beah gifan. þ hi sceoldon begen on burh  
ridan hale to hame oððe on here     292  
crincgan on wæl stope wurðum

ſpelcan he læȝ ðeȝenlice ðeoðne ȝe-
henðe. ða peaſð bopða ȝebpæc bpimen
poðon ȝuðe ȝeȝpemoðe ȝaſ ofc þuph poð.   296
fæȝes feophhus fopða eoðe piscan þuſ-
ſcaneſ ſuna pið þaſ ſecȝaſ feahc he
pæs onȝeþpanȝ hÿpa þpeopa bana æp hi
piȝelineſ beapn on þa pæle læȝe. þæſ   300
pæſ ſcið ȝemoc ſcoðon fæſce. piȝan on
ȝepinne piȝenð cpuncon punðū pepiȝe
pæl feol on eopþan. Oſpolð 7 eaðpolð eal-   304
le hpile beȝen þa ȝebpoþpu beopnaſ cpÿ-
meðon hÿpa pinemaȝaſ popðon bæðon
þ hi þæp æc ðeapfe þolian sceolðon un-
paclice pæpna neocan. Bÿphcpolð maþe-   308
loðe boſð hafenoðe se pæſ ealðȝeneac æsc
acpehce he ful balðlice beopnaſ læſðe.
hiȝe sceal þe heapðpa heopce þe cenpe   312
moð sceal þe mape þe upe mæȝen lÿclað.
heſ lið uſe ealðoſ eall foſ heapen ȝóð on
ȝpeoce amæȝ ȝpopnian se ðe nu fſa þiſ   316
piȝ pleȝan penðan þenceð. ic eom fpoð
feopeſ fſa ic ne pille ac ic me behealfe
minū hlafopðe be ſpa leofan men licȝan
þence. ſpa hi æþelȝapeſ beapn ealle bÿlðe   320
ȝoðpic to ȝuþe oft he ȝaſ foplec pælspepe
pinðan on þa picinȝaſ spa he on þa folce
fÿpmeſc eoðe heop 7 hÿnðeoð þ he on hilðe   324
ȝecpanc næſ þ na ſe ȝoðpic þe ða ȝuðe fopbeah . . . .

# REVIEW OF SELECTED ARTICLES AND BOOKS

## 1726

**HEARNE, Thomas**: *Johannis Confratris et Monachi Glastoniensis Chronica*, (Oxford) vol.2 pp.570–577

An edition of John of Gastonbury's *Chronicle*, which also contains the first printed version of the text of *Maldon*, and the one all subsequent editions were based on up to 1937. The printing was made from the Bodleian transcript, and introduced further errors from misreading of the handwriting there e.g. **hugende** for **hicgende**, line 122. Vol.I p.li contains a brief note on the transcript.

## 1786

**GOUGH, Richard**: *Sepulchral Monuments*

Vol.1 pt.1 p.clvi and plate opposite shows seated frontal portrait of Byrhtnoth, from the reign of Edward III, copied and printed here prior to restoration of the choir at Ely which obliterated the original drawings, while Byrhtnoth's bones were re-interred in Bishop West's chapel.

## 1877

**ten BRINK, B.**: *Geschichte der Englischen Litteratur*, (Berlin) vol.I

Suggests (p.145) that *Maldon* represents a religious or spiritual conflict, with Byrhtnoth in the role of a Christian martyr.

## 1882

**ZERNIAL, U.**: *Das Lied von Byrhtnoths Fall. 991*, (Berlin)

Early study of the poem with translation of text into alliterative modern German verse, and discussion of word-meanings, style etc.

## 1892

**JESPERSEN, Otto**: "Små randnoter til engelske texter", *Nordisk Tidskrift för Filologi* ser.3, vol.I (1892–3) pp.126–130

Suggests Hearne's *gemunu þa* in line 212 could go back to a MS. form *gemunaþ ā*.

## 1894

**FITCH, E.A.**: *Maldon and the River Blackwater* (Maldon)
Contains a spirited rhyming-couplet translation of *Maldon* on pp.8–11.
Notes on many points of local interest. "Few relics of the Saxon or Danish
period have been discovered here. Saxon urns and coins (sceattas) have
occurred in several localities, but most commonly at Heybridge."

## 1898

**LIEBERMANN, F.**: "Zur Geschichte Byrhtnoths, des Helden von
Maldon", *Archiv für das Studium...* vol.101 pp.15–28
Reviews the historical sources on Byrhtnoth's life and the background to the
poem including later Latin accounts; places *Maldon* firmly in the realm of
history.

## 1904

**SEDGEFIELD, W.J.**: *The Battle of Maldon and Short Poems from the
Saxon Chronicle* (Belles Lettres series, Boston & London)
An edition of *Maldon* with apparatus covering earlier editorial variants,
brief notes and glossary. Also an interesting introduction, in which he posits
"the awakening and development of a new form of epic narrative" in the late
10th century – "plain, blunt, stern" (vi–vii); and gives translations into
English of the medieval Latin texts mentioning Maldon, e.g. the *Liber
Eliensis* account.

## 1905

**KLAEBER, Frederick**: "On Certain Passages in Old English Historical
Poems", *Modern Language Notes* vol.20 pp.31–32
Minor comments (p.32) on Sedgefield's translation.

## 1910

**HOLTHAUSEN, Ferd.**: "Zur altenglischen literatur", *Anglia Beiblatt*
vol.21 pp.12–14
For line 109, suggests adding *grimme* before *gegrundene*, cf. *Ruin* line 14
*grimme gegrunden* and *Otuel* verse 57 *grymly grownden gare*. For lines 15
and 237, suggests compounds *bradswurd* and *godswurd*; completes line 172

with *hæleð gemælde*; emends *on bord* in line 270 to *to borde*; prefers the forms *modlice* in line 200, *genehhe* in 269.

## 1917-18

**HOLTHAUSEN, Ferd.**: "Zu altenglischen Denkmälern", *Englische Studien* vol.51 pp.180-188
To regularise alliteration in line 224 prefers "he wæs min ægðer mæg and hlaford" to Ettmüller's *mandryhten* for *hlaford* in b-verse.

## 1919

**EMERSON, Oliver F.**: "Notes on Old English", *Modern Language Review* vol.14 pp.205-219
Suggests *spillan* line 34 means "spend ourselves" rather than "destroy each other"; *unorne* line 256 means "simple, plain" rather then "worn out, old".

## 1920

**KOCK, E.A.**: Notes in *Anglia* vol.44 p.248
Suggests *wigan* in line 126 should be taken as a noun (paralleling *men* in line 125), rather than as a verb.

## 1921

**KLAEBER, Frederick**: "Zu Byrhtnoþs Tod", *Englische Studien* vol.55 pp.390-395
Some of the warriors on Byrhtnoth's side seem to have Viking i.e. Danish names, and could have been men of Essex of Danish descent e.g. Gadd (line 287), Maccus (line 80), and Þurstan (line 298). Other possible Viking elements are *dreng* (line 149) and *sprengde* "twisted" (line 137).

**KOCK, E.A.**: Notes in *Anglia* vol.45 p.123
Points out that *afysan* in line 3 is a transitive verb applying to the horses not an intransitive verb applying to the men.

## 1924

**LABORDE, Edw.D.**: "The Style of *The Battle of Maldon*", *Modern Language Review* vol.19 pp.401-417
Looks at (a) variation (b) ornamental epithets (c) poetic formulas (d) parenthetic clauses (e) vocabulary (where poetic words seem fairly rare,

and compounds are less frequent than in *Beowulf*, identified as Scandinavian by source are *wicing, griþ, dreng, eorl* and *ceallian*) [but is this last West Saxon?] – and (f) syntax (more unaccented 'empty' words than in *Beowulf*, tendency to end sentence at end of line than centre). The result, a simple, plain, but arguably developed and mature style.

## 1925

**LABORDE, Edw.D.**: "The Site of the Battle of Maldon", *English Historical Review* vol.40 pp.161–173
Examining the evidence of the text (lines 25, 28, 57–8, 63, 65–6, 68, 72, 74–5, 77–8, 81, 87–8, 91, 96, 97–8, 193–4), localises the battle on that part of the Blackwater where the channel is narrow enough to shout across but tides still act (the upper tidal limits are Beeleigh on the Chelmer, Heybridge on the Blackwater; below Northey the river is perhaps too wide and deep to fit the action of the poem). Freeman had previously located the battle at Heybridge, where there was a bridge or crossing; but this is above Maldon, and the Vikings would risk having their retreat cut off and their boats burned if they fought inland of the fortified town. Also, there would be alternative crossing-places near Heybridge, not envisaged in the text. Rather, *bricg* in the poem (since *ford* is also used) should be taken to mean simply 'dry crossing', and then the site fits Northey Island well. Laborde notes the causeway there as some 80yds long, 8 feet wide (narrower once?) and sided by impassable mud. An inland ridge (where now a road runs from the causeway to South House) may have marked Byrhtnoth's position; Godric's flight was probably south west towards Hazeleigh (though an area now deforested).

## 1927

**BRETTY, Cyril**: "Notes on Old and Middle English", *Modern Language Review* vol.22 pp.257–264
On lines 46–8, notes that *heregeatu* does not mean simple 'war-gear' but 'heriot', a sort of tax or customary payment – "this 'heriot' is the dead man's best possession, often a sword, which passes to his lord by law and custom." (p.260).

## 1929

**KLAEBER, Frederick**: "Jottings on Old English Poems", *Anglia* vol.53 pp.227–229
Notes the irony in lines 55ff, and compares them to *Beowulf* 430. Suggests a simple opening for the poem:
«Ær se burhstede abrocen wurde...»
Its ending, he feels, could either have been simple and short (like the Cynewulf and Cyneheard episode in *Chronicle A 755*), or more positive and triumphant like the *Bjarkamál*. In either case, "the fact of defeat vanishes before the self-sacrificing heroism of the *comites*." (p.228).

**PHILLPOTTS, B.S.**: "*The Battle of Maldon*: Some Danish Affinities", *Modern Language Review* vol.24 pp.172–190
Surviving Old English historical/battle poems sited in or related to the Danelaw: could the inspiration for this genre of poem be Viking? The sort of heroic value esteemed in *Maldon* is comparable to a Danish runic epitaph from the 980s or a little later, which translates as "This (man) fled not at Uppsala, but fought while he had weapons." (p.176). Old English *Brunanburh* resembles the Old Norse poem on the Battle of Hafrsfjörð; *Maldon* has much in common with Saxo's surviving Latin version of the Danish *Bjarkamál*, a poem also dealing with a heroic stand after the death of a leader.

## 1930

**ROWLES, Henry J.**: *The Battle and Song of Maldon,* (Colchester 1930)
Translation into modern alliterative-style verse; short general introduction.

## 1937

**DICKINS, Bruce**: "The day of Byrhtnoth's death and other obits from a twelfth-century Ely kalendar", *Leeds Studies in English* vol.6 pp.14–24
A Winchester kalendar (Cotton MS. Titus D.xxvii ff.3–8b) of perhaps the early 11th century gives Byrhtnoth's date of death as 11th August; the 12th century kalendar (Trinity College Cambridge MS.O.2,1), gives the date 10th August; though later, this second authority was written at Ely which is intimately connected with Byrhtnoth.

## (1937)

**GORDON, Eric V.**: *The Battle of Maldon* (Methuen's Old English Library)

The first edition to use the Casley transcript. A thorough introduction covers the site of the battle, the Latin records, the probable error in *Chronicle A* 993, Byrhtnoth's career, the heroic tone of the poem, the Cotton MS. (the first half, including *Maldon,* said to be late 11th century and probably from Worcester; the second half perhaps 12th century and from Barking); the transcript (which is accepted as an accurate representation of the MS.); and the language (westernised forms of an originally eastern counties text?). The text (with substantial footnotes) is printed in long lines without a central cæsura. A glossary follows.

**GORDON, Eric V.**: "The Date of Æthelred's Treaty with the Vikings: Olaf Tryggvason and the Battle of Maldon", *Modern Language Review* vol.32 pp.24–32

The Anglo-Saxon Chronicle mentions two treaties with the Vikings in the 990s: (a) in 991 after Maldon; this was apparently a local treaty (worth £10,000) arranged by Archbishop Sigeric for the benefit of some of the eastern counties; and (b) in the autumn of 994, a more general treaty. The text of one treaty between Æthelred and Anlaf does survive, and its general scope and large value (£22,000) suggest it is the 994 rather than the 991 treaty. If so the Anlaf it mentions (Ólafr Tryggvason, later king of Norway) need not have been present at Maldon; the later accounts of Florence of Worcester and the *Liber Eliensis* name Justin and Guthmund as the Viking leaders there.

**LABORDE, Edw.D.**: *Byrhtnoth and Maldon*

An edition of the poem, based on Hearne. Introduction includes sections on the characters (with useful lists of Byrhtnoth's estates pp.23–4, 34–5), the battlefield (identified, with map and photos, as near Northey Island in the estuary of the Blackwater, "originally a drowned valley"), and a survey of the external records (in Latin only). Text follows: in line 16 *þa* is emended to *þæt* by analogy with line 291 [a good though not essential alteration], and line 172 is filled out to "wigendra hleo, he to heofenum wlat".

# 1938

**BROWN, Carleton**: *"Beowulf* and the *Blickling Homilies* and some Textual Notes", *PMLA* vol.53 pp.905–916
On pp.909–10, notes resemblance between fleeing warriors in *Maldon* and deserters in Beowulf's last fight.

**WOOLF, Henry B.**: "The Personal Names in *The Battle of Maldon*", *Modern Language Notes* vol.53 pp.109–112
Looks at familial alliteration amongst the names of relatives preserved in the poem, and finds examples of traditional patterns of linked sound in them.

# 1950

**KLAEBER, Frederick**: *Beiträge zur Geschichte der deutschen Sprache u. Lit.* vol.72 pp.128–129
Suggests (re line 297+) that Wigel(m) and Thurstan are alternative names for the same man (Wistan's father), and that the second name is Danish-based. For line 189, calls *þe ahte* etc. a "Skandinavismus".

# 1952

**LAWS, F.H.**: *Maldon a Thousand Years Ago*
Pamphlet with list of translations; summary of the poem; local and historical background material.

**MEZGER, F.**: "Self-Judgment in Old English Documents", *Modern Language Notes* vol.67 106–109
Self-judgement is where "the defendant was allowed to fix his own damages, compensation, etc." (p.106). Considers other probable references in Old English (e.g. *Genesis* 1900ff) and Old Icelandic.

# 1953

**BRITTON, G.C.**: *Times Literary Supplement* 27 Feb. (=p.137)
Letter to the Editor, suggesting *ofermod* likelier to mean 'great, high courage' than 'over-confidence'.

**TOLKIEN, J.R.R.**: "The Homecoming of Beorhtnoth, Beorhthelm's son", *Essays & Studies* n.s. vol.6 pp.1–18

Contains (i) a short introduction on the poem (ii) an alliterative verse play on the supposed recovery of Byrhtnoth's body after the battle (iii) a note on *ofermod* (line 89) which he translates as 'overmastering pride' – which might in certain circumstances be regarded as heroic or at least defended as 'noble', but in this case "Byrhtnoth was wrong, and he died for his folly."

## 1954

**SUDDABY, Elizabeth**: notes in *Modern Language Notes* vol.69 466–467
Re *Maldon* line 190b "þe hit riht ne wæs", considers *þe hit* as combined relative, or *þe* as dative ("on those trappings"), but prefers emendation to *þeh* 'though'; cf. *neh* line 103, and lines elsewhere in Old English poetry at *Genesis A 901* and *Chronicle C* for 1036.

## 1956

**FUNKE, Otto**: "Some Remarks on Late Old English Word-Order", *English Studies* vol.37 99–104.
Against Quirk & Wrenn's *Grammar*, demonstrates that word-order in *Maldon* is not prosaic as assumed of late poetry, but that the verb preserves much of the flexibility of position expected for it in traditional Old English poetry.

**KUHN, Hans**: "Die Grenzen der germanischen Gefolgschafte", *Zt. der Savigny-Stiftung für Rechstgeschichte*, (Germanistische Abteilung) vol.73 pp.1–83
Looks at the history of the Germanic *comitatus*, from Tacitus (whose evidence might however refer more to Celtic society) to 10th century Anglo-Saxon England (where the concept might have been a Viking introduction). Notes (p.15) that *þegn* describes a member of a comitatus, and could by origin mean 'youth' (cf. Greek τεκνον 'youngster' – though other words based on *þegn* in Old English relate to 'service'); and (p.44–5) suggests that *hīrēdmen* (line 261) has not Old English sense of 'household' but Norse sense of 'retinue, comitatus' (i.e. *hirð*).

## 1960

**WHITEHEAD, Frederick**: "**Ofermod** and **desmesure**", *Cahiers de Civilisation médiévale* vol.3 pp.115–7
Doubts Tolkien's interpretation of *ofermod* as 'pride' – if defeat is Byrhtnoth's fault, what merit would there be in the loyalty shown him by

his *heorðwerod*? The context is explored in terms of comparison with the Chanson de Roland.

## 1961

**IRVING, Edw.B.Jr.**: "The Heroic Style in *The Battle of Maldon*", *Studies in Philology* vol.58 456–467.

Assumes *Maldon* written soon after event – a sort of "medieval journalism" (p.458) with a "powerful sense of verisimilitude". Example of proof, that to have two Godric's, one good one bad, would be too clumsy in fiction. Rather, *Maldon* is "the classic statement, the pure essence, of the Germanic heroic ideal" (p.458). Of Byrhtnoth's invitation of the Vikings to the mainland, says it was "tactically... a disastrous example of stupidity" (p.462) and the correct course would have been to contain the Vikings on the island and to starve them out. Analyses the poem in stages. Prefers comma to full stop after *eorðan* (line 233).

**MAGOUN, Francis P.**, Jr.: "Some Notes on Anglo-Saxon Poetry", *Studies in Medieval Literature in Honor of Prof. A. C. Baugh (Philadelphia)* pp.273–283

Looks at the theme of "the gesture of the raised shield and/or brandished spear" in *Beowulf* 235–6, *Maldon* 42–4, 230, 244–5, 255, 309–10; in all cases occurs before speech "to give solemnity" [i.e. literary weight?] to what follows.

## 1962

**BESSINGER, J.B.**: "*Maldon* and the *Óláfsdrápa*: An historical caveat", *Comparative Literature* vol.14 pp.23–35

An important warning against taking the *Maldon* text too literally: such poems "are no more truthful than they should be" (p.24). "The fresh urgency of the narrative... proves that the poem is skilfully contrived, not that it is an accurate report." (p.25). In *Maldon,* dates and place-names are basically lacking, and the landscape is not necessarily accurately portrayed e.g. 'west' in line 97 could be part of an alliterative block rather than an exact direction. Could the Anglo-Saxons have prevented the Vikings departing by ship? – probably not (p.31). Need the Vikings indeed have been on an island at all? The *Óláfsdrápa* (ca.AD 1001) is similar to *Maldon* in its inexactness, but sinks into an unstoic indulgence in grief at Óláf's death. "Historical poems like these are only secondarily about events." (p.35).

## (1962)

**BLOOMFIELD, Morton W.**: "Patristics & Old English Literatures: Notes on some Poems", *Comparative Literature* vol.14 pp.37–38
On *Maldon* lines 175–80 (end of Byrhtnoth's prayer, where he hopes his soul will elude the demons), notes that this image was an established theological neurosis e.g. used by Gregory the Great (*PL* vol.76 col.1298).

**ELLIOTT, Ralph W.V.**: "Byrhtnoth and Hildebrand: A study in heroic technique", *Comparative Literature* vol.14 pp.53–70
How did the Vikings *lytegian* – since Byrhtnoth has previously shown he is not easily duped? (p.57). Was he perhaps taunted with cowardice? Notes that in *Hildebrandslied* a different impasse similarly resolves itself into fiercer fighting. Praises the style of *Maldon*.

**GILLAM, D.M.E.**: "The Connotations of Old English *fæge*: with a note on Beowulf and Byrhtnoth", *Studia Germanica Gandensia* vol.4 pp.165-201
An interesting study of a word by context, deducing that (a) the word is used principally of humans (good and bad) (b) it implies the imminence of death (c) it implies the operation of external forces e.g. fate or God. It is not used of Beowulf or Byrhtnoth, since great men are not held to be subject to "powers outside and beyond their control". On p.186, notes that once in battle a shield-wall had been disrupted, either for pursuit or because of attack, the battle must inevitably resolve itself into a number of hand-to-hand encounters.

**HOLLISTER, C.** Warren:*Anglo-Saxon Military Institutions on the Eve of the Norman Conquest* (Oxford)
Studies the Anglo-Saxon *fyrd*, which he divides into two types: the 'great fyrd' or every freeman's liability to take up arms and serve at least in local defence; and the 'select fyrd', a rationalisation of the above, by which one permanent soldier serves for and is paid from each 5 hides of land. The personnel of the 'select fyrd' would equal "thegns and well-armed peasants", and these, plus Byrhtnoth's personal retainers (whom he counts as a paid or mercenary group) may have constituted the army at Maldon, not

the 'great fyrd'. The evidence for a professional soldiery grows stronger during the 11th century, but need not apply [I think] to the 10th century.

## 1963

**SAMOUCE, W.A.**: "General Byrhtnoth", *Journal of English & Germanic Philology* vol.62 pp.129–135
A military analysis of *Maldon*: Byrhtnoth is faced with three options: (i) to retreat and avoid battle; (ii) to prevent the Vikings landing from Northey so they give up and sail away; (iii) to go for pitched battle, as a victory would prevent "further attacks by the Norwegian force... [and] avenge the previous sackings of Folkestone, Sandwich and Ipswich." (p.131). 11th August 991 – probably a warm day, and so Byrhtnoth's men would have been tired already by marching to the battle-site – they may have been "merely a hastily assembled levy." (p.132). It is possible that the Vikings were numerically superior – "Attack on commanding terrain is normally predicated on a superiority of strength." (pp.132–3). Byrhtnoth's troops were ranged north-south on flat land, with emphasis on shield-wall defence; he could not seek a better (higher) position without losing contact with the Vikings; his real advantage lay in attacking the Vikings as they crossed the water, and this he gave away "because of the ethics of his time" (p.134).

## 1965

**BATTAGLIA, F.J.**: "Notes on *Maldon*: Toward a definitive **ofermod**", *English Language Notes* vol.2 (1964–5) pp.247–249
Reviews interpretations of *ofermod*; in view of the context ("tricked" line 86, "yielding too much land" line 90), concludes that *ofermod* must be derogatory; and therefore *Maldon* cannot be considered a eulogy to Byrhtnoth.

**BLAKE, N.F.**: "The Battle of Maldon", *Neophilologus* vol.49 pp.332–345
Suggests that *Maldon* has features in common with a saint's life narrative i.e. vagueness with respect to place-names, and presentation of physical conflict in terms of a spiritual one – thus Vikings in *Maldon* portrayed as tricky and devilish [but Cross 1965 disagrees]. In particular, in Ælfric's Life of *St. Edmund* (written 996–7) the Vikings are shown as "heathen, devilish and malicious anti-Christians" (p.335), while Edmund, like Byrhtnoth, resolutely defies a Viking emissary and rejects submission. If so, *Maldon* cannot be taken to be critical of Byrhtnoth and *ofermod* is explained by

analogy with *wlenco* in *Beowulf* 338, which there means "exuberance" though elsewhere in Old English, "pride".

**BRITTON, G.C.**: "The Characterization of the Vikings in *The Battle of Maldon*", *Notes & Queries* vol.210 pp.85–87

Apart from the "crafty insolence" (p.86) of the Viking herald, the Vikings are not individualized but rather treated as a group, "animalized" (p.86) through the epithet *wælwulfas*, while other terms e.g. *scealcas* could also be derogatory [but Cross 1965 disagrees]; if so, there is much "emotional force" (p.87) or bias displayed by the poet.

**CROSS, J.E.**: "Oswald and Byrhtnoth", *English Studies* vol.46 pp.93–109

Byrhtnoth, dying in the Christian cause, could be literally considered a martyr, cf. Oswald, who died in battle. Yet their motives seem different: Oswald is concerned with Christian goals in a war to defend/establish Christianity; Byrhtnoth's ideals are Germanic, and *Maldon* "a secular poem... with the aim of illustrating secular virtues and motives." (p.109). Demonstrates that the epithets applied to the Vikings are not all or necessarily derogatory, so that *Maldon* as good versus bad and Byrhtnoth as a martyr seem less likely.

## 1966

**JOHN, Eric**: *Orbis Britanniae* (Leic.Univ.Press) pp.133ff

Argues against a national *fyrd* composed of *ceorlas* (freemen) in favour of a "selective *fyrd*" of well-equipped thanes (into which class it is assumed Dunnere the ceorl must fit); therefore (pp.292–3) denies any meaningful distinction between *folc* and *heorðwerod* in *Maldon* e.g. Godric, who flees, is not apparently a ceorl.

**MILLS, A.D.**: "Byrhtnoð's Mistake in Generalship", *Neuphilologische Mitteilungen* vol.67 pp.14–27

Suggests that whatever qualities Byrhtnoth may have possessed as a commander, he committed "one fatal tactical mistake in the battle... he gave up a strong and virtually impregnable strategic position for the uncertain outcome of pitched battle." (p.15). Byrhtnoth is seen as gullible (p.23) and an inexperienced soldier (p.24). Could the taunt from the Vikings which made Byrhtnoth yield them space have been a religious one, daring him as a Christian to come to battle and let God decide the issue?

## 1967

**CLARK, Cecily**: "Byrhtnoth and Roland: A Contrast", *Neophilologus* vol.51 pp.288–293

Contrasts Byrhtnoth's and Roland's deaths: Roland prays for his comrades, confesses his sins and admits to his own failure in battle; Byrhtnoth more "selfish" (p.289) in his final prayer. Roland's war more explicitly Christian versus pagan; Byrhtnoth aims only to defend "Æþelredes eard" (line 53). *Maldon* therefore a secular poem concerned with Germanic heroism in the tradition of Tacitus.

## 1968

**CLARK, George**: "The Battle in *The Battle of Maldon*", *Neuphilologische Mitteilungen* vol.69 pp.374–379

Defends the poem's "mosaic of battle images" (p.375) – coherence comes from concentrating on Byrhtnoth in Pt.1, and diverging into individual cameos in Pt.2 – reflecting the reality of the battle. Notes that Wulfmær, by withdrawing the spear that killed Byrhtnoth from the body, "thereby obligated himself to avenge his lord's wound" (p.375).

**CLARK, George**: *"The Battle of Maldon*: A Heroic Poem", *Speculum* vol.43, pp.52–71

In *Maldon,* ostensibly the good die and the bad survive; but there must have been some other purpose to Byrhtnoth's insistence on battle than simply to invite defeat. If interested only in defending Maldon or Essex, then Byrhtnoth could have simply held the ford until the Vikings gave up and sailed off – and let the other shires take their chance. But the Byrhtnoth of the poem takes upon himself the defence of the kingdom, and so must proceed to battle.

**HALE, David G.**: "Structure and Theme in *The Battle of Maldon*", *Notes & Queries* vol.213 pp.242–243

Analyses *Maldon* as (a) lines 1–184 "affirmation of the Germanic moral order", (b) lines 185–259 "a serious challenge to this order" (i.e. from Godric's flight), (c) lines 260–324 "a concluding reaffirmation of the heroic code".

## (1968)

**SWANTON, Michael J.**: *"The Battle of Maldon*: A Literary Caveat", *Journal of English and Germanic Philology* vol.67 pp.441–450
A particularly provocative and necessary article. Suggests that there is discord between the "social structure implied in *Maldon*" and what we know of late 10th century society – could the poem therefore have been written "as a deliberately nostalgic exercise intended to embarrass the corruption of Æthelred's court"? (p.443) i.e. the poet could be invoking the standards of Tacitus' *Germania* [ch.13–14] without regard to the difference between a pre-Christian war-band and Byrhtnoth's 10th century army. Re *superne*, line 134, suggests that this word could have connotations of calamity as much as of direction.

## 1969

**BLOOMFIELD, Morton W.**: "Beowulf, Byrhtnoth, and the Judgment of God: Trial by Combat in Anglo-Saxon England", *Speculum* vol.44 pp.545–559
Did Byrhtnoth invite the Vikings to a fair fight in order to leave the decision on the victory to God? There is no certainty that the concept of trial by combat was present in England before the Conquest, so it is also possible that the poet was criticising Byrhtnoth for invoking God in this context.

**BOLTON, W.F.**: "Byrhtnoth in the Wilderness", *Modern Language Review* vol.64 (1969) pp.481–490
Conjectures that Pt.1 of *Maldon* could be seen as a series of temptations, to which Byrhtnoth finally succumbs by reason of his *ofermod*. (If so, the Vikings play a demonic role.) Since the Church Fathers permitted rearrangement of detail for interpretive effect, perhaps therefore *Maldon* "implements a historical incident to provide for its readers an instance of the moral pattern archetypically represented by the temptations of Christ in the desert." (p.489).

**CAMPBELL, Brian R.**: "The suþerne gar in *The Battle of Maldon*", *Notes & Queries* vol.214 pp.45–46
*Suþerne gar* (line 134) refers either to a "spear... thrown from the south" or "a spear of southern make" – here the latter preferred, cf. *francan*, a Frankish or southern spear in lines 77 and 140. The *suþerne gar* that wounds Byrhtnoth could indeed have been an Essex spear, thrown in the

exchange of missiles in lines 108–112, picked up by a Viking and now returned. If so a sort of paradox is involved, a challenge to the "deadly ghost of heroism which haunts *The Battle of Maldon*" (p.46).

## (1969)

**REANEY, P.H.**: *Place-Names of Essex* (EPNS vol.12)
Notes that *Pant* [the name means "valley" in Celtic] was formerly used of the whole river but today only of that stretch above Bocking, that below being called the Blackwater; though locally the estuary is still sometimes referred to as *Pont* or *Pant*. The same name is used of a small stream flowing through South Hanningfield to join the Chelmer (p.251) and may have been the original name of the Stour (p.451).

**STANLEY, E.G.**: "Old English '–calle', 'ceallian'" , *Medieval Literature & Civilization: Studies in Memory of G.N.Garmonsway*, ed. D.A.Pearsall & R.A.Waldron pp.94–99
*Hildecalle* (*Exodus* line 252) could be an Anglian rather than Viking form.

## 1970

**ANDERSON, Earl R.**: "The Flyting in *The Battle of Maldon*", *Neuphilologische Mitteilungen* vol.71 pp.197–202
Deals with lines 25–61; notes contrast between Viking herald's emphasis on the undesirableness of battle and the desirableness of peace, and Byrhtnoth's rousing response; the contrast between the Viking herald's use of *þu* – isolating Byrhtnoth – and Byrhtnoth's use of *hi* and *we* in reply. Looks at the "incongruous collocation" (p.199) of *gafole* and *garas* (which can be compared to *Hildebrandslied* lines 33–8), and other examples of word-play in the *Maldon* flyting.

**HILL, T.D.**: "History and Heroic Ethic in *Maldon*", *Neophilologus* vol.54 pp.291–6
Seems to suggest (p.295) that *Maldon* was written as a restrained or oblique criticism of Byrhtnoth.

**MACRAE-GIBSON, O.D.**: "*Maldon* – The Literary Structure of the Later Part", *Neuphilologische Mitteilungen* vol.71 pp.192–196
Considers the reasons behind the order of the "heroic vignettes" in Pt.2: these emphasise different aspects of loyalty, "with the most elaborate speech first" (p.194) – or by order of the (increasing) age of the speakers – or by

shift of emphasis from theme of vengeance to theme of death. Suggests the poem could have ended in no more than two more lines:

«He, Oddan bearn, earglice fleah;
he and his geferan fuhton oþ swulton.»

## (1970)

**MACRAE-GIBSON, O.D.**: "How Historical is *The Battle of Maldon?*", *Medium Ævum* vol.39 pp.89–107
Reviews site of battle – only two suitable islands Osea (which has the longer causeway) and Northey. If Northey, then the shore (*ofre* line 28) on which Byrhtnoth formed his battle-line might not be the water's edge (which are now marshes or 'saltings') but a natural ridge a little inland (formed by London Clay). On 10th August AD 991 low tides are assessed to have occurred at 4.30am and 5pm; battle might thus have commenced about 4.30pm; sunset was at 7.30pm.

**METCALF, Allan A.**: "'West' in *Maldon*", *Papers on Language & Literature* vol.6 pp.314–322
Whether "west over the Pante" is factual or not, it could be taken to indicate aggression on the part of the Vikings, to whom 'west' meant the interior of England and 'east' retreat over the sea.

## 1973

**KOLB, Eduard**: "Battle of Maldon 183: An emendation", *English Studies* vol.54, p.618
For line 183b suggests *wegen lagon* – 'lay killed' for source's *begen lagon*.

## 1974

**CROSS, J.E.**: "Mainly on Philology and the Interpretative Criticism of *Maldon*", *Old English Studies in Honour of John C. Pope*, ed. Rob.B.Burlin and Edw.B.Irving Jr, (Toronto) pp.235–253
In fact mostly about Clark's assertions of 1968. Marshalls evidence to confirm that *lytegian* and *ofermod* should be interpreted as critical of Byrhtnoth.

## 1975

**McKINNELL, John**: "On the Date of *The Battle of Maldon*", *Medium Ævum* vol.44 pp.121–136
Supposes *eorl* (used only of Byrhtnoth in *Maldon)* to be a title (e.g. line

203) and therefore equivalent to Old Norse *jarl*. But *eorl* only used of an English *ealdorman* after Cnut's reorganisation of government in 1017. If *Maldon* does in fact date from Cnut's reign, this might explain problems other critics have had making sense of the factual content of the poem.

**SKLAR, Eliz. S.**: "*The Battle of Maldon* and the Popular Tradition: Some rhymed formulas", *Philological Quarterly* vol.54, pp.409–418
Argues that there are many irregularities in *Maldon* that show the poet was losing touch with traditional techniques e.g. fewer compounds, weakening of mid-line caesura etc. Not necessarily lack of skill, for this could show the influence of an alternative popular poetic tradition, anticipating the Early Middle English works *Proverbs of Alfred, Worcester Fragments* and *Layamon's Brut.*

## 1976

**BLAKE, N.F.**: "The Flyting in *The Battle of Maldon*", *English Language Notes* vol.13 pp.242–5
Notes on special use of pronouns in exchange between Viking herald and Byrhtnoth.

**GNEUSS, Helmut**: "*The Battle of Maldon* 89: Byrhtnoþ's *ofermod* once again", *Studies in Philology* vol.73 pp.117–37
Does *ofermod* mean pride, overconfidence, rashness, courage or magnanimity? The prefix *ofer–* can mean "great" as well as "excessive", but *ofermod* elsewhere in Old English always denotes "pride" and is likely to do so here too. Perhaps Byrhtnoth was deliberately risking battle to avoid the Vikings simply sailing away and ravaging elsewhere. A good intention, but Domesday Book for Essex suggests *fyrd* could have been as few as 550 warriors.

**GNEUSS, Helmut**: *Die Battle of Maldon als historisches und literarisches Zeugnis*, Bayerische Akademie der Wissenschaften, Phil.-Hist. Klasse, Sitzungsberichte (Munich) vol.5
Summary of poem; section on concept of 'retinue' (*comitatus*), which he relates to practice in 9th and 10th century Danelaw rather than Tacitus; and section on the poem itself, with special consideration of its context in the

lost MS. Otho A.xii, which might have been produced in Kent or Essex, and perhaps at Barking Abbey.

## (1976)

**MILLS, Carl R.**: "Stylistic Applications of Ethnosemantics: Basic color terms in *Brunanburh* and *Maldon*", *Language and Style* vol.9 pp.164–170
Though intensely visual, *Maldon* makes relatively little use of colour, Anglo-Saxons being more interested, it seems, in shades of light and dark, surface sheen etc.

**PETTY, George R. & PETTY, Susan**: "Geology and *The Battle of Maldon*", *Speculum* vol.51 pp.435–446
Took core-samples from the causeway to assess its history, and deduced that the channel could have been narrower then (120 yds as opposed to the present 240 yds?), with firmer, steeper banks where there are now saltings. If so, the battle-site is now marsh at best.

**ROBINSON, Fred C.**: "Some Aspects of the *Maldon* Poet's Artistry", *Journal of English & Germanic Philology* vol.75 pp.25–40
1. Reckons that Viking herald's speech (lines 29–41) could be first example of literary use of dialect in English e.g. *grip, garræs, þon* ("than") etc.. 2. Are the references to Æthelred ironic? If so, composition of *Maldon* could relate to period of disillusionment with that monarch AD 999+. 3. Re *ofermod*, wonders if the Viking island could have held English prisoners, hence Byrhtnoth's unwise longing for a decisive battle. 4. *wæl–* compounds surely derogatory of Vikings. 5. *Wiges heard* (line 130) could apply to Byrhtnoth or a Viking – perhaps an omission in the text here. 6. *þe hit* (line 190) better if *þeah* for *þe*; there could have been a MS. page-break here, hence copying error. 7. Ælfwine's speech (lines 212–24) has emphasis on first-person verbs, so *gemunu* could be right (cf. Late West Saxon *ic gemune*) and no need to convert to an imperative. 8. Does *forheawen* (line 314) represent the decapitation of Byrhtnoth, or is the poet avoiding this topic, wishing not to focus on the brutality of the Vikings but on the heroism of the English? 9. *eald geneat* (line 310) could imply age or simply experience. This speech of Byrhtwold is paralleled in Widukind of Corvey's *Rerum Gestarum Saxonicarum Libri Tres* of about AD 973, where Hathgat, also an old man, raises the standard and rallies the others: "If the fates do

not allow me to live longer, let me at least – for this is dear to me – lie at last among my comrades..."

## (1976)

**WOOLF, Rosemary**: "The Ideal of men dying with their lord in the *Germania* and in *The Battle of Maldon*", *Anglo-Saxon England* vol.5 pp.63-81
Denies any direct link between Tacitus and *Maldon* – Tacitus may indeed have been talking not about Germans but Celts, seeking only to idealize barbarians. By Byrhtnoth's own day, the Germanic *comitatus* would have been a meaningless concept in a "stable Christian society"; yet it is not impossible that Tacitus' *Germania* was known in England and inspired the poet, since Tacitus was read in monasteries like Fulda in the 9th century. Alternately, and more probably, the source of the ideals in *Maldon* is to be sought among the Danes and in works like the *Bjarkamál*.

## 1978

**BLAKE, N.F.**: "The genesis of *The Battle of Maldon*", *Anglo-Saxon England* vol.7 pp.119–129
First author to place importance on the *Vita Oswaldi* account; assumes *Maldon* actually later in date of composition than the Latin and perhaps even based on it; *Maldon's* apparent fact-content could be purely literary elaboration, including causeway, names, the Northumbrian hostage etc. The tides and Byrhtnoth's actions then become devices of literary tension, and the poem is seen as the product of a (monastic) cult of Byrhtnoth in East Anglia in the 11th century.

**BZDYL, D.G.**: "Prayer in Old English Narrative", *Olifant* vol.5 pp.373-375
Report of thesis (see also *DAI* vol.38 no.6 p.3473–A); Byrhtnoth's prayer is seen neither as flawed nor as especially saintly, but simply marks the hero as a good Christian; its literary role may be more important...

**DOANE, A.N.**: "Legend, History and Artifice in *The Battle of Maldon*", *Viator* vol.9 pp.39–66
Deplores polarization into literal acceptance/rejection of *Maldon* text, seeing *Maldon* as a 'chanson de geste'. Points out that lost MS Cotton Otho A.XII

comprised texts of figures "notable for their military and political efforts against the Danish marauders." (p.50)

## 1979

**CLARK, George**: "The Hero of *Maldon*: Vir Pius et Strenuus", *Speculum* vol.54 pp.257–282

Criticises Tolkien and Cross for basing interpretation of whole poem on single words or lines; in the end it is Godric's flight not Byrhtnoth's decisions that lose the battle. The size of the armies cannot be clear; a Viking raiding force might have 6–10 ships, 50–60 men a ship; the Essex fyrd could provide about 550 men if one man from every 5 hides, but many more if one man from each hide. All the external evidence points to the high esteem Byrhtnoth was held in. Therefore challenges that *ofermod* is critical or in critical context – *lytig* can mean "astute" as well as "underhand" and need not imply that Byrhtnoth was tricked.

## 1981

**BUSSE, W.G. & HOLTEI, R.**: "*The Battle of Maldon*: A Historical, Heroic and Political Poem", *Neophilologus* vol.65 pp.614–621

Looks at the way the loyal survivors of Byrhtnoth take their decisions, and how they evolve, though leaderless, a "communal way of acting", although the group has no regional, social or hierarchical coherence. These thanes, it is suggested, are the true heroes of *Maldon*, and the poem's political aim could be to urge concerted action by the thane-class where higher authority [i.e. Æthelred?] had failed.

**SCRAGG, D.G.**: *The Battle of Maldon* (Manchester Univ. Press)

A new edition, on the lines of Gordon's (1937). Introduction covers the MS., the transcript, the historical background (*heorþwerod* is not seen as foreshadowing the housecarls or professional bodyguard of Cnut's time), language ("consistently close to the late Old English standard of Winchester" (p.25), though does not mean the poem was written in Wessex; any of the monasteries patronised by Byrhtnoth might be the source of the poem); and structure (considers *ofermod* critical of Byrhtnoth but the poem supportive of Byrhtnoth). Text is printed without vowel length indications. There is a commentary, bibliography and glossary.

# 1982

**BZDYL, D.G.**: "Prayer in OE Narrative", *Medium Ævum* vol.51 pp.135-151
Considers Byrhtnoth's dying prayer in context of OE devotional prayer structure, and its consequent limitations as character evidence.

**ROBERTS, Jane**: *"Maldon* 189b: þe hit riht ne wæs", *Notes & Queries* vol.227 p.106
On the analogy of *Andreas* lines 507 and 630, suggests that the disputed *þe* in *Maldon* line 189 could be "a reduced form" of *þeah* i.e. stand for *þeah* without emendation. Could this also apply to *þe* in line 313?

**STUART, Heather**: "The Meaning of *Maldon"*, *Neophilologus* vol.66 pp.126–137
As against "historical" or "heroic" interpretations, aims to look at *Maldon* as "an independent artistic entity" (p.126) indeed labels *Maldon* an "antiheroic" [i.e. satirical?] poem.

# 1983

**CLARK, Cecily**: "On Dating *The Battle of Maldon*: Certain evidence reviewed", *Nottingham Medieval Studies* vol.27 pp.1–22
*Eorl* in its special sense used only of Viking leaders in 9th century e.g. *Parker Chronicle* 871; not used more generally of any shire leader until about the 1010s. But this need not mean a later date for *Maldon,* if a Southern Danelaw provenance is accepted for the poem [e.g.Ely?]; there *eorl* "leader" would naturally come into common use earlier than in Wessex. Confirms that Thurstan, Gadd, Maccus (Irish Viking) and perhaps also Wistan and Odda, are all likely to be Viking names in origin; but such 9th century settlers integrated into the English by late 10th century, along probably with some of their words [cf. Robinson 1976 on dialect].

# 1984

**FLETCHER, A.J.**: "Cald wæter, scir wæter", *Neuphilologische Mitteilungen* vol.85 pp.435–437
Sees these two adjectives (lines 91, 98) as conveying feeling and intimating the eventual outcome of the battle.

**LOCHERBIE-CAMERON, Margaret A.L.:** "Two Battles of Maldon", *Trivium* vol.19 pp.55–59
Investigates the Latin accounts, and proposes possibility that they telescoped two battles, one in 921, one in 991.

**SCATTERGOOD, John (ed.):** "*The Battle of Maldon* and History", *Literature and Learning in Medieval and Renaissance England* (Essays presented to Fitzroy Pyle) (Blackrock) pp.11–24
Summary of scholarly opinion for and against the factual accuracy of the poem. By Chronicle quotations, he shows the relevance of the Danegeld debate and the risks of desertion in battle in the 1000s and 1010s just as much as the 990s.

## 1985

**HILLMAN, Richard:** "Defeat and Victory in *The Battle of Maldon*: The Christian resonances reconsidered", *English Studies in Canada* vol.11 pp.385–393
How can Byrhtnoth be a hero and lose? Only, it is averred, in Christian terms, where success is measured on a different scale. Notes (p.392) that 12 retainers plus the coward Godric are mentioned, and compares line 325 to John 14.22 (the two Judas's).

**ROGERS, H.L.:** "*The Battle of Maldon*: David Casley's transcript", *Notes & Queries* vol.230 pp.147–155
Transcript (Bodleian Rawlinson B.203), ascribed to Elphinston by Thomas Hearne, shown to be the work of David Casley (who succeeded Elphinston as deputy keeper of the Cottonian Library in 1718). This demonstrated by examples of handwriting. Other transcripts by Casley show that he was somewhat careless, inconsistent in his copying of letter-forms, accents, abbreviation and punctuation marks, and liable to misread letters. Many features of the transcript are thus not to be depended on (e.g. authentic line-division, hooked "e" etc.). The readings *leofne* (line 7), *laþe* (line 86), *west* (line 97), *gearo* (line 274) are confirmed as Casley's, and several emendations based on probable misreading of letters become the more likely.

# 1986

**FRESE, D.W.**: "Poetic Prowess in *Brunanburh* and *Maldon*: Winning, Losing, and Literary Outcome" , *Modes of Interpretation in Old English Literature: Essays in Honour of Stanley B. Greenfield* ed. Phyllis R.Brown et al. (Toronto) pp.83–99
Argues for *Brananburh* to be accorded some equivalence of status with *Maldon* and "its dazzling varieties of impersonated consciousness" (p.83): both are re-worked from history, indeed the moral themes in *Maldon* can be found in various *Chronicle* entries, 991–1003.

**PARKS, Ward**: "Flyting and Fighting: Pathways in the Realization of the Epic Context", *Neophilologus* vol.70 pp.292–306
The flyting or verbal contest considered in the larger context of comparative literature e.g. Viking herald compared to *Iliad* XX, 178–352.

**VALENTINE, Virginia**: "Offa's *The Battle of Maldon*", *Explicator* vol.44 no.3 pp.5–7
Is the hawker at the opening of *Maldon* being cool or frivolous? Could the two Offa's of the poem make a contrast (like the two Godric's)? But this first Offa is not really being rebuked; he is merely showing high spirits, and sets things to right himself as soon as he realises "what is appropriate".

# 1987

**EVANS, D.A.H.**: "*Maldon* 215", *Notes & Queries* vol.232 pp.5–7
Looks at the alternative translations for line 215: "now one can find out who is brave"/"now the one who is bold can put it to the test"; rejects the second, as *cunnian* means "test, find out", not "show, demonstrate".

# 1988

**LOCHERBIE-CAMERON, M.A.L.**: "Byrhtnoth, His Noble Companion and His Sister's Son", *Medium Ævum* vol.57 pp.159–171
Argues for the authenticity of detail in the poem and thus an early date of composition.

## 1989

**BALL, Christopher**: "Byrhtnoth's Weapons", *Notes and Queries* vol.234 pp.8–9
Notes that *gar* (p.138), *ord* (p.146) and *swurd* (p.166) in Byrhtnoth's response to the Viking herald also represent the weapons of Byrhtnoth's three encounters with Vikings, in the actual fight, in that order, suggesting that detail in the poem is literary rather than literal.

## 1991

**SCRAGG, Donald (ed.)**: *The Battle of Maldon AD991* (Oxford)
Includes facsimile of transcript of text, edited text and a facing translation; a bibliography; and short articles on '*The Battle of Maldon*' by Donald Scragg, 'The *Anglo-Saxon Chronicle*' by Janet Bately, 'The *Life of St. Oswald*' by Michael Lapidge, 'Byrhtnoth's Obits and Twelfth-Century Accounts of the Battle of Maldon' by Alan Kennedy, 'The Historical Context of the Battle of Maldon' by Simon Keynes, 'The Danish Perspective' by Niels Lund, 'English Tactics, Strategy and Military Organization in the Late Tenth Century' by Richard Abels, 'Æthelred's Coinage and the Payment of Tribute' by Mark Blackburn, 'The Site of the Battle of Maldon' by John McN.Dodgson, 'Byrhtnoth's Eighteenth-Century Context' by Kathryn Sutherland, *'The Battle of Maldon* and Heroic Literature' by Roberta Frank, 'Weapons and Armour' by Nicholas Brooks, 'Hawks and Horse-Trappings: the Insignia of Rank' by Gale R.Owen-Crocker, 'The Men Named in the Poem' and 'Byrhtnoth and his Family' by Margaret A.L.Locherbie-Cameron, 'The Byrhtnoth Tapestry or Embroidery' by Mildred Budny, 'Byrhtnoth's Tomb' by Elizabeth Coatsworth, 'Byrhtnoth's Remains: a Reassessment of his Stature' by Marilyn Deegan and Stanley Rubin, and 'A Bibliography of the Battle of Maldon' by Wendy E.J.Collier. Reviewed by Eric Stanley in *Notes & Queries* vol.237 (1992) pp.79–83.

**NORTH, Richard**: "Getting to know the General in *The Battle of Maldon" Medium Ævum* 60 pp.1–15
Speculates that *Maldon* was written in the 990s to protect Byrhtnoth's posthumous reputation - was the poet covering up for "obscene hecklers" on the Danish side, who moved Byrhtnoth to rash action?

# 1992

**WALLIS, S.**: "Maldon Landfill Site", *Essex Archaeology and History* vol.22 pp.167–170
Notes on an excavation in land 400m. from assumed site of battle; but with no finds relevant to the battle or its period.

**BREEZE, Andrew**: "Maldon 68: Mid prasse bestoden", *English Studies* vol.73 pp.289–291
Suggests *prass* (line 68) might mean "physical crowd" rather than abstract "pomp", by comparison with Welsh "pres".

**BREEZE, Andrew**: "Finnsburh and Maldon: *celæs bord, cellod bord*", *Notes & Queries* vol.237 pp.267–269
Could *celæs* and *cellod* equal *celced*, 'lime-washed'? Such whitened shields are evidenced in the Gododdin ('calch') and in Irish literature ('cailc'), ultimately from Latin'calc–'; and would make good sense in context in both *Finnsburh* and *Maldon*.

**STANLEY, E. G.**: "OE 'ær' conjunction: 'rather than'", *Notes & Queries* vol.237 pp.11–13
Argues that OE 'ær' is not purely temporal, but can often better be translated 'rather than' e.g. at *Maldon* line 61.

# 1993

**COOPER, Janet (ed.)**: *The Battle of Maldon: Fiction and Fact* (London)
Contributions include the following:

**James Campbell**, "England, c.991" (pp.1–17)
Looks at monastic background of the time, as possible setting for composition of *Maldon*, if a funeral song to be performed at a commemoration of Byrhtnoth's death.

**Donald Scragg**, "*The Battle of Maldon:* Fact or fiction?" (pp.19–31)
Supports C10th date for poem on basis of spelling of first element in name *Byrht*-noð (p.28), though evidence includes unstressed -*berht* forms. Achievement of poem lies in unsurpassed skill "in the creation of character." (p.24) Narrative may not be literally true, but need not be

invented either (p.23) – rather it is faithful at a higher level, as demonstrated via parallels in Tennyson. (pp.29–31)

**Peter Sawyer**, "The Scandinavian Background" (pp.33–42)
Sees Maldon as a upsurge of Danish activity 950 AD on: leading Viking figure (if any) in battle likelier Svein than the Norwegian Olof.

**Paul E. Szarmach**, "The (Sub-)Genre of the *Battle of Maldon*" (pp.33–42)
Examines OHG (rhyming) poem, 'Ludwigslied', and Latin (hexameter) 'Bella Parisiacae Urbs', both of late C9th, as possible evidence (with *Maldon*) of a move towards the chanson de geste genre. (p.61) En route affirms *ofermod* as 'pride'.

**Ute Schwab**, "*The Battle of Maldon:* A memorial poem" (pp.63–85)
Asserts the fidelity of some detail (e.g. Byrhtnoth's wounds, p.73), but sees speeches as fictitious, within a Germanic framework (comparisons include funeral dirges and the *Heliand*). Perhaps those named in the poem were chosen for inclusion by the patrons of the poet? (pp.80–83) Even more interestingly, could the structure and idiosyncracies of the poem be explained by transfer from another medium? (p.84) Specifically, muses that Ælfflæd's tapestry might be the source of the poem – a fascinating possibility in view of the two-part structure, and limited background detail on characters.

**Karl Leyser**, "Early Medieval Warfare" (pp.87–108)
Explores known Viking tactics, which included a variety of 'tricks' such as hiding in woods, attacking at night, and using ambushes.

**Niels Lund**, "Danish Military Obligation" (pp.109–126)
Asks whether Danish attacks were spontaneous raids or planned state campaign e.g. were Viking warriors supported by taxation at home? Concludes that such organisation likelier in C11th. (p.126)

**George and Susan Petty**, "A Geological Reconstruction of the site of the Battle of Maldon" (pp.159–169)
Reaffirms history of site as supportive of the poem. Formerly, a narrower channel and firmer banks are posited.

**Cyril Hart**, "Essex in the Late Tenth Century" (pp.171–204)
Uses Doomsday Book to recreate earlier economic conditions, leading to suggestion that Colchester and Maldon only became important as boroughs in the 990s.

**D.M.Metcalf and W.Lean**, "The Battle of Maldon and the Minting of Crux Pennies in Essex: *Post Hoc Propter Hoc?*" (pp.205–224)
Though both Colchester and Maldon acted as mints from before the date of the battle, there was an upsurge of coin production in approximately 991. Did this reflect some growth of the towns (and trade) consequent on a release of land after Byrhtnoth's death, or were the coins specifically minted to pay danegeld?

**Pauline Stafford**, "Kinship and Women in the World of *Maldon:* Byrhtnoth and his family" (pp.225–235)
Reflects on the curious situation that only female relatives of Byrhtnoth have left traces in charters, yet the poem names only men. Perhaps Byrhtnoth came from Wessex and married into an Essex family? (p.229) On the question of Wistan (lines 297–300) named as both Thurstan's son and Wigelm's *bearn*, suggests a more fluid use of the term 'bearn' than just direct offspring. (p.226)

**Roberta Frank**, "*The Battle of Maldon:* Its reception, 1726–1906" (pp.237–247)
Though the text of *Maldon* was printed in 1726, it received little attention until included in Conybeare's 1824 *Illustrations of Anglo-Saxon Poetry*. Since then it has engendered much scholarly interest, but remained (remains?) unappreciated by a wider public.

**STORK, N.P.**: "*Maldon*, the Devil, and the Dictionary" *Exemplaria* 5 pp.111–134
Elaborates interpretation in which Vikings play the role of demons, seeking not only Byrhtnoth's death but his soul.

## 1994

**ANDERSON, Earl R.**: "The Roman idea of a *comitatus* and its application to *The Battle of Maldon*" *Mediaevalia* 17 (1994 for 1991) 15–26
The "principle of reciprocity" did not necessarily include suicidal loyalty; indeed the *comitatus* would originally have been a Roman concept

promulgated to strengthen leadership and weaken kinship and the tribe. In this view, *Maldon* "is not a historical document".

**FRESE, D.W.**: "'Worda and worca': *The Battle of Maldon* and the lost text of Ælfflæd's tapestry" *Mediaevalia* 17 (1994 for 1991) 27–51
In terms of the emphasis on the action of speaking and the division into short distinct scenes, links the Bayeux tapestry and the *Maldon* poem with the seminal Maldon tapestry, gifted by Ælfflæd, Byrhtnoth's widow, to Ely Abbey, "a hanging woven and figured with the deeds of her husband in memory of his excellence" according to the *Liber Eliensis*.

**HILL, John M.**: "Transcendental loyalty in *The Battle of Maldon*" *Mediaevalia* 17 (1994 for 1991) 67–88
Attributes the loyalty shown by Byrhtnoth's closest retainers as Christian in impulse, an inversion of "survival-orientated responses" and the traditional search for secular glory.

**NILES, John D.**: "Maldon and mythopoesis" *Mediaevalia* 17 (1994 for 1991) 89–121
Aims to counter arguments that *Maldon* is critical of Æthelred.

## 1995

**CAVILL, Paul**: "Interpretation of *The Battle of Maldon* lines 84–90: a review and reassessment" *Studia Neophiloligica* 67 pp.149–164
Attempting to "make some sense of the three cruces" (*lytegian, landes to fela, ofermod*).

**CREED, R.P.**: "*The Battle of Maldon* and Beowulfian prosody" pp.23–41 in *Prosody and poetics in the Early Middle Ages: Essays in honour of C.B.Hieatt* ed. M.J.Toswell (Toronto)
*Maldon* lines confirm to *Beowulf* patterns except lines 1, 29, 32, 45, 80, 172, 183, 224, 240, 271 and 288.

**GRIFFITHS, M.S.**: "Alliterartive licence and the rhetorical use of proper names in *The Battle of Maldon*" pp.60–79 in *Prosody and poetics in the Early Middle Ages: Essays in honour of C.B.Hieatt* ed. M. J. Toswell (Toronto)
Studies the metrical and semantic role of personal names in the text.

# 1995

**LOCHERBIE-CAMERON, M. A. L.**: "Some things the *Maldon* poet did not say" *Parergon* 13.1 pp.69–80
Analyses *Maldon* as a eulogy of Byrhtnoth. The "laconic or prosaic" reporting may not have seemed so to contemporaries, aware of "resonances" that give a depth of context.

# 1996

**HOUGH, Carole**: "*The Battle of Maldon* lines 20–21" *Neuphilologische Mitteilungen* 97 pp.383–386.
Proposes *rand* (accusative singular) for *randan* in line 20.

# 1997

**HILL, T.D.** "The *Liber Eliensis* 'Historical Selections' and the OE *Battle of Maldon*" *Journal of English and Germanic Philology* 96 pp.1–12.
Notes that OE *ofermod* parallels Latin *nimia...animositate*, and proposes a lost mutual source, an oral Maldon 'saga'. Prefers "a single 'two-part' battle" to "two distinct battles" (p.5) and attributes the two battles in the *Liber Eliensis* to misunderstanding of the two panels of the tapestry.

**PHILLIPS, Helen**: "The order of words and patterns of opposition in the *Battle of Maldon*" *Neophilologus* 81 pp.117–128.
Studies "word ordering which enacts aspects of the physical events it describes."

**PULSIANO, Phillip**: "'Danish men's words are worse than murder': Viking guile and *The Battle of Maldon*" *Journal of English and Germanic Philology* 96 pp.13–25.
A re-examination of lines 84–90. Was Byrhtnoth indeed a victim of Danish smooth talking?

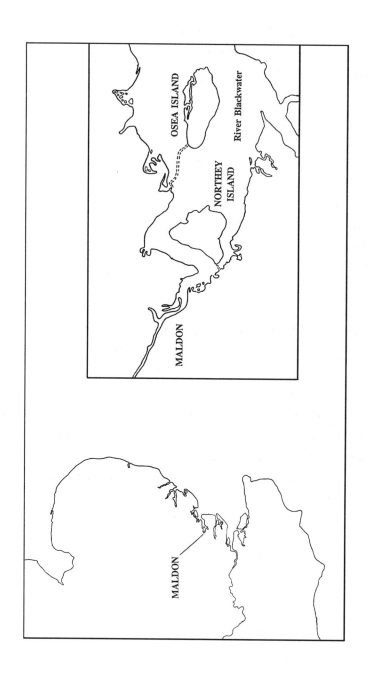

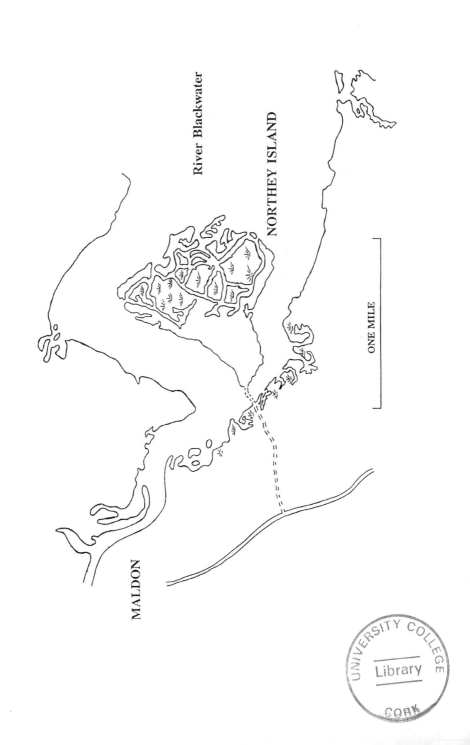

River Blackwater

NORTHEY ISLAND

MALDON

ONE MILE